One Writer's Way

One Writer's
Way

by
ELIZABETH YATES

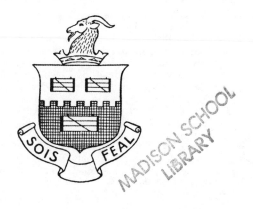

THE WESTMINSTER PRESS
PHILADELPHIA

BOOK DESIGN BY DOROTHY ALDEN SMITH

First edition

Published by The Westminster Press ®
Philadelphia, Pennsylvania

PRINTED IN THE UNITED STATES OF AMERICA
2 4 6 8 9 7 5 3 1

Library of Congress Cataloging in Publication Data

Yates, Elizabeth, 1905–
  One writer's way.

  SUMMARY: Based on the author's diaries for the years 1931 through 1951, traces the development of her career as an author of children's books while her husband, after losing his sight, becomes a leader in organizations for the blind.
    1. Yates, Elizabeth, 1905–   —Biography.
2. Authors, American—20th century—Biography.
3. Children's literature—Authorship. 4. McGreal, William. 5. Blind—United States—Biography. [1. Yates, Elizabeth, 1905–   . 2. Authors, American.
3. McGreal, William. 4. Blind. 5. Physically handicapped] I. Title.
PS3547.A745Z474 1984   818'.5209 [B] [92]   83-26044
ISBN 0-664-32712-5

CONTENTS

1931
16, WYTHBURN COURT

January, 1931

Much as I love England and much as it means to both of us, I feel a little uneasy quiver and ask Bill if we will be here all our lives. He assures me that "ninety-nine years" in the lease is a formality, that there is a clause tucked into the wording which says a lease can be assigned any given year.

Four addresses in a little more than a year! On the last lease, for 16, Wythburn Court, the wording is elegant. It sounds like Shakespeare, and there is not a mark of punctuation in the whole two pages. That is the way with a legal document in England. It must be stated in such a manner that the ideas are independent of punctuation and cannot be misunderstood.

Looking Back

Bill McGreal's quarters in Mayfair were right enough for cozy bachelor living, but not "for gracious living," as Mother said when she and Father came to visit us in London early in the year. Bill won their hearts just by being himself, and the time sparkled with dinners at the Savoy, theaters, concerts, shopping. When we saw them off on the boat train for Paris, it was with a relationship secured and sure, and we promised them that we would soon have more of a home to live in.

We heard of a small house in Kensington that could be rented furnished for six months, and soon moved into it. There was little to move but our clothes and books, some china and linen that we had been acquiring. Friends in America, family, and relatives had been sending us checks for wedding presents, so that when the time came for us to furnish our own home we would be able to. What good fortune! We would not have to make do with what people thought we would like, but could get what we really liked, needed, and would use. The exchange from dollars to pounds, with the rate approximately five dollars to the pound, was simple even for my arithmetic.

Number 24, Victoria Grove was a charming little Huguenot house with a small garden. We had a daily maid, and for the (to me) utterly unfair wage of a pound a week I felt freed to spend a good part of my days exploring London, Baedecker in hand. Of course, I did the food shopping, enjoying it immensely once I got accustomed to seeing the great carcasses at the butcher shops and wild birds with their feathers at the poulterer's. At the greengrocer's one day I commented on the high price of beans. "Never you mind, lady," was the comforting reply. "I'm doing a bean at ninepence tomorrow; come back then."

From Maude I learned to be explicit, to show her, not just to tell her, what was wanted. A certain Sunday morning I had planned a special treat for Bill—lamb kidneys on toast, and breakfast not until nine o'clock. When the kidneys appeared, they resembled little black marbles. I asked Maude about them, and she said she had cooked them when she arrived at seven o'clock. She seemed as surprised as I was annoyed at their appearance. "But, madam," she said, "I did them with love in my heart." Later I shared my woe with Bill. He had an antidote. "God will tell the little girl." It was one of his sayings, and in the face of frustration and vexation it calmed me down.

Spring, 1930

Spring came early, but never too early to leave the damp, shivering days of winter behind, and April meant that Sinna could be part of our life again. Bill's company had loaned him a car for two weeks to visit branches in the southwest, and our first stop was at the kennels in Hackbridge, Surrey. Greeting us, the kennelman said, "That little dog! He's been quiet and good ever since he came here last November, but what did he do last night? He set up such a barking that all the other dogs joined in. It was bedlam for sure; but if you're asking me, he knew you were on your way to fetch him. Good little fellow, and a fine Sealyham he is. He served his time fairly, but when he knew it was near over, he had to tell everyone."

Sinna welcomed us extravagantly, then settled into the car with his eyes ahead and not so much as a backward glance at the kennels.

And we were off.

To drive through the English country in the spring of the year is to see green hillsides dotted with the whitest of lambs and roadsides bright with primroses. Stopping by a little stream for our picnic luncheon, I heard the cuckoo for the first time; and then the sky-lark, losing itself in the blue above us. It was just like Shelley's poem that I had learned at school:

> Higher still and higher
> From the earth thou springest
> . . . .
> And singing still dost soar,
> And soaring ever singest.

"Tonight we may hear the nightingale," Bill said.

We did, from a woodland glade, rising like an aria above the accompaniment of waves crashing against the rocks far below us.

We stayed three days and nights at Lee Abbey on the Devon coast, where we had spent our first Christmas. Then it was holly thick and tall, the prickly leaves changing to smooth near the top where the berries grew in abundance, and ivy trailing up old walls—the same holly and ivy that I had sung about in Christmas carols and never dreamed to see actually growing. We took walks along the coast and inland on the moors. The warmth of the sun was balanced by the frequent mists that rolled in from the sea and often turned to rain, but rain was so usual that it never meant any change of plans for us, and Sinna relished all weather. Returning to the inn always meant tea by a fire of great logs.

This is Lorna Doone country, familiar to me from reading about it in the days when I never thought I would be a part of it. On our way into Lynmouth one morning, we watched a hunt gathering at The Blue Ball. The red coats, the handsome horses, the impatient dogs, the sounding of the huntsman's horn were all exciting, like the pages of a book coming to life; but, as I watched them coursing up the Vale of Watersmeet, I

10

hoped with all my heart that the fox would get away. Bill wasn't so agitated as I was, he merely reminded me in that gentle way of his that we must take people as they are. "The English have always gone in for fox hunting, even though there's no nation on earth kinder to animals. Some things you can't change, so don't use yourself up trying to."

At Lee, that lovely old abbey become an inn, I learned how simple it was to travel with a dog in England. At the bottom of our bill, when we came to leave, was Sinna's. It matched him in size.

With the first months of our first year of marriage, I felt that I was drinking in a whole new way of life and people—in London against the backdrop of museums and libraries, plays and antiquity; in the country against the backdrop so well described by Trevelyan as "delicate and fugitive beauty, made up of small touches, a combination of nature with the older arts of man." Impressions came quick and fast, and I jotted them down in my notebook to sort out later. Bill, in love with his camera, was taking pictures, never the usual ones, but scenes that caught his eye and had stories to tell.

Summer, 1930

We spent a week in the New Forest visiting the Paget-Cookes. There we acquired a puppy, Bara, named after our hostess Barbara. He was no more than a little ball of mirth and mischief, but we knew that someday he would grow into being a dignified Scottish terrier. We worked it out logically: we had each other, Sinna needed someone.

There was an unforgettable day when Bob's book

arrived. *When I Was a Harvester* is real, and now it will be on its way through stores and libraries into the minds of readers and into their hearts, too. It reminds me of what I hope to achieve someday—but "When?" I keep asking myself. Writing, except in my journal, isn't the focus of life it once was. The days have been so filled with new experiences, and curious things keep happening that take up my time and delight me.

One such happening is the suit Bill wanted me to have made at Bradley's. It meant several appointments, which took up a great deal of time. When it was finished and I wore it for the first time, I felt like royalty. Another happening has been going to Miss Edith Clements for voice lessons, at Bill's insistence.

"But why, Bill? I have no intention of ever becoming a singer."

"You'll be a speaker all your life," he said, and then went on to persuade me of the importance of good enunciation, of deep breathing, and much more.

Until I began to work with Miss Clements, I had not realized how careless I was, how often I slurred a word instead of giving it its due. For years I've been particular about the written word; the spoken word is fully as important. It was through Miss Clements that I met Miss Marguerite Puttick, who has a school for children in Kensington. There was an extra plum when I went to Miss Clements, in that her flat was near Madame Tussaud's. After a lesson, I often visited the waxwork figures and practiced my new techniques in conversation with them. But the real prize was inquiring at Liberty's the price of silk pajamas for Bill and being told in pounds and shillings rather than in dollars and cents.

Autumn, 1930

When our lease ran out at Victoria Grove, we found another furnished house, number 8, Canning Place. It was a very little house, old and damp, with the only warmth coming from coal fires and a hot towel rail in the bathroom. I knew more than ever how important it was to have a maid, and not only for the fires but to clean the silver weekly, especially the tea service that Bill's company had given us. Fog tarnished it, and when autumn came fog was everywhere, even seeping in through keyholes. I was cold then, trying to write with a hot-water bottle on my lap for my hands and a coal fire at my back. But there was another kind of cold.

One day, getting home in the late afternoon when dusk and chill had taken over the London streets, Elsie opened the door to me with her finger on her lips. "The master is upstairs. Something is wrong. He wanted the curtains drawn—" I did not wait to hear the rest. The door to our room was closed. I opened it and knelt beside the bed. Bill was lying there, a cloth over his eyes. "It's just the pain," he murmured. "Light. Noise. They're like knives."

For two weeks it was like that. Keeping the room as dark as I could, and as quiet, was the only palliative. Even the doctor knew no other way to alleviate this kind of pain. "It will pass," Bill said, and it did. "It may not come again for a long time." But when it came again, he knew—and I had been told—that the price would be a degree of sight. He made light of it: he would—it was his way. The day he went back to his

13

office happened to be our anniversary. That afternoon a box came from the florist, twelve red roses and a card in that exquisite handwriting of his, "Darling, it has been a year of sweetness and joy. You are precious indeed. B."

Twelve red roses. Elsie brought me a tall vase and as I placed them in it I wondered, as I had on other occasions, how a heart could break at the same time with happiness and with anguish. The strength and beauty of the roses filled the room as their fragrance did. I tucked myself into a chair by the fire to read, but when Elsie brought me tea, I put the book away and let my thoughts move with the flames as they circled the shiny chunks of coal.

And I saw that just as the flames released the essence of the coal, so love was doing that to me and to Bill. It was making each one of us something more. I give to Bill and he gives to me—it is an equality—and we each give to life. Determined as I had been to gain my independence when I moved away from the family circle, I did not surrender it through marriage. I gained in finding happiness; and yet I know that happiness doesn't just happen. It is something to be worked at constantly. It may mean hard work, but what doesn't mean that? Growing up was not easy, nor was growing into love.

Elsie came in with the dogs from their usual evening walk.

"Will you be wanting anything more, madam?"

"No, Elsie. Thanks. We're going out to dinner and the theater. I'll see you in the morning."

And that was my reminder to stop dreaming by the fire and go up to change. It would be evening dress for me, white tie and tails for Bill and that marvelous top hat which worked with a spring and went as flat as a pancake when he got into a taxicab. We were going to celebrate at the Piccadilly Hotel, where we had had breakfast a year ago, and we had seats in the stalls to see Dame Sybil Thorndike in *Saint Joan.*

Winter, 1930

During the next few weeks, much happened. Bill learned of a new block of flats, Wythburn Court, just off Bryanston Square. If we took one, we could have it decorated to our taste. I went to Heal's on Tottenham Court Road and had the joy of choosing what we needed in carpeting and curtains, then essential furniture. All of it was done with the discreet suggestions of a Mr. Warrington, and I learned a great deal from him about colors and fabrics. The flat had central heating. That meant the chill was taken off the air. A coal fire in the living room gave real warmth.

With Mrs. Charles Balmain, my first friend in England, I went shopping in earnest. My guideline was that whatever was purchased must meet our present need, be beautiful, and be sturdy enough to serve for a long time. Bill was firm about that. What we got would not be temporary, but for life. There was a long-established furniture store in Esher, and there we went several times. Mrs. Balmain knew antiques—the makers, the history—and she had a feeling for detail. A piece might look to be in good condition, but her searching fingers could find a defect if there was one; and her eye, like an ear with perfect pitch, knew what was authentic.

We chose a dining room table, mahogany, oval, right for six people, with a leaf to extend it for more.

Its date was 1789, and it came from a house in the Midlands where it had served long and been well cared for. The grain was handsome. "Wash it with soap and water, give it a rub of oil now and then, and it will serve you well," we were told. Six chairs went with it, quite as old, and their damask seats were frayed and faded. Their design was in Sheraton's notebook, and it thrilled me to think of all they had witnessed in their lifetime.

To these we added a small tilt-top table for tea, like the kind often seen in Zoffany portraits of the period, a dresser, a desk, a low sofa table that had come from a parsonage. These were the nucleus. Other pieces would be added—beds, comfortable chairs, and a plain table for me to use. Before we left, the clerk made out a sales slip that had not only the prices but the dates.

"You'll need it for the customs when you return to America."

At that time I could not imagine our ever returning, and yet in my heart I knew that sometime we would.

So the checks that had come from friends and family did this for us, exactly to our taste and our need.

By mid-December Elsie's room was finished and the kitchen was equipped. The flat was full of the smell of paint and plaster, and all the furniture had to be cleaned and polished when it arrived from Esher, so we made a lightning decision to go to Spain for Christmas rather than spend the time getting settled. Elsie would take care of the dogs, wash china, put books on shelves, and do a hundred small things. She was as excited about her part as we were about our escapade.

To Málaga was two days and nights on a P. and O. liner, and our cabin was really posh. I learned the

16

meaning of a word often used casually—Port Out, Starboard Home was the comfortable way to travel when people were bound for India. When I had my first sight of Gibraltar, the Gates of Hercules, I felt that I was with Ulysses.

Then Christmas! Last year it had been so very English—holly and ivy, a great tree strung with lights, a Yule log on the fire, roast beef, and a flaming plum pudding, and poppers as part of the table setting. At the proper moment they had been opened, people had snapped them and put the paper hats on their heads. It was all rather ritualistic, as if it were being done that way because it had always been done that way. The huge hotel in Málaga, once a palace, had all the Christmas trimmings and something lighthearted and unpredictable. There was spontaneous laughter and talk in many languages, the least to be heard was English; there was dancing, and it didn't seem to matter who whirled whom about as everyone was there to have fun.

We had a week of warm sunny days, visiting by foot and sometimes by charabanc much of southern Spain. Then two days home on the S.S. *Viceroy of India,* and the sea in the Bay of Biscay was very rough.

Two weeks away was enough to send Bill to his office impatient to catch up with his work, and me to the small room that had nothing in it but the table, a straight chair, and a shelf for books. There were several letters from America, but two I took very much to heart. Loyola Sanford, editor and friend, said, "Don't fret that you are not writing yet. You are growing into a whole new way of life, and any growing takes time. I know you are not one to lose your dream. It has led you too long." Eunice Stephenson, artist and friend, said, "In spite of all the good things that have filled your letters, I think this year has had some loneliness for you, with Bill away so much of the day and the reserve of the English to counter. Much as I love hearing from you, don't write yourself out in letters. Perhaps it's time now to sharpen your pencil."

Spring, 1931

Springtime comes again, if not always in the air, then with the flower sellers on the street corners—anemones and violets from Cornwall, narcissus and daffodils from the Scilly Isles; and the days are so much longer.

There is a smooth routine now to the pattern of my life. After a morning at home, I take the dogs for a brisk walk around Bryanston Square, then down Wimpole Street, where I pass with a fast-beating heart Number 50, the house from which Elizabeth Barrett slipped secretly one night to be married to Robert Browning in Marylebone Church. Elsie has luncheon for me and then I'm off —often to spend the afternoon in the great circular Reading Room of the British Museum. The buff-colored card that has to be renewed every six months and that gives me entrance is one of my most precious possessions. Evenings are for and with Bill. Sometimes it will be a theater, more often it will be reading aloud and talking by the fire, with the dogs always near.

I had been making needlepoint seats for our dining room chairs. The pattern is beautiful and it follows the Licorne Series of medieval tapestries. In each one there is a royal lady and her attendant, a lion and a unicorn, many small animals, flowers and trees, and each depicts one of the five senses. The sixth, *Mon Seul Désir,* is that which tells of her marriage. In my mind, as I worked, I was writing a story about this. It was slow stitchery, for the colors are many and subtle and they change often. I set myself a year for each piece.

In the British Museum, it wasn't all reading. Sometimes I wandered around the art rooms. One day I was permitted to hold in my hands a folio of William Blake's work, the very drawings he had made! Long have I loved *Glad Day* and when I held it in my hands, it fairly sang to me from the paper and made me echo inwardly Louis Untermeyer's words—

> Come day, glad day, day running out
>   of the night
> With breast aflame and your generous
>   arms outspread;
> With hands that scatter the dawn and
>   fingers busy with light,
> And a rainbow of fire to flicker about
>   your head.
>
> Come soon, glad day, come with the
>   confident stride
> Of the sun in its march over
>   mountains, of the wind on its
>   way through the air.

Recently I'd been deep in books by and about George Eliot, especially her letters and John Walter Cross's biography of her. So real she became, I thought I saw her one day in her long black cape and with her deep sad eyes. I felt some poignant kinship and wanted to write about her to bring her ideals and greatheartedness alive again. Bill was away for a week, so I took the train to Coventry to walk in her footsteps. The house where her growing-up years were spent, when she was Mary Ann Evans, can be visited. I was allowed to sit at her desk, to handle and read some of her letters, then to see the school she attended during her "tempestuous teens." She yearned so for perfection and loved those who symbolized it.

March, 1931

Eunice said, "Don't stop dashing off those fascinating letters from the British Museum. Your creativeness and industry are operating through them, and I can see a certain style developing in the more temperate climate of England. You've always been instinctively drawn to the great minds of the ages, and I'm not surprised that you spend so many happy hours in that Reading Room. We all seek the experiences we need in order to grow, any healthy organism does this, and you are taking from people, events, and the life around you what you need for your growing."

I sent Loyola a brief word sketch of George Eliot and she replied, "I am proud of you and the writing you are doing. Your style is improving. You express your ideas with far more clarity and force. Things are moving in you and before long they will move for you. Don't you have the feeling that you can go anyplace in the world, for your career is in you? Your letters are filled with the joy of living. Write out of that."

Now that gave me an idea: perhaps I should write a story as if it were a letter, and then, when I come to revise it, simply eliminate the salutation and the farewell.

My reading desk at the British Museum gave me the bliss of solitude, a relief after the big gatherings Bill and I had to attend sometimes. They were very formal, and my whole soul seemed to quiver and curl within me at the thought of being among so many people. I kept thinking that if there were just one person with whom I could talk seriously about things that matter, not just cheerless chitchat, everything would be all right. I never have liked big functions. I never will.

When Bill and I entertained at Wythburn Court, the groups were small. There were only six chairs in our dining room, and the table, without the leaf, seated just that number, and six is a right number for conversation. Bill comforted me and told me to be myself, but to remember that no matter how unapproachable a person may seem, there is always some point of contact that can be found. "See it as a challenge," he said.

April, 1931

Mrs. Balmain was earnest about introducing me to the real London, things I should see and know about, not as a tourist, but as a resident. During Holy Week she took me to the Maundy Thursday Service at Westminster Abbey, when King George actually did wash the feet of a dozen poor men. She found a reason to come up to London from Ashtead about once a week, and that meant we met in Green Park for a walk with the dogs, then went to the Army and Navy Stores for tea. In the entry there was a place where dogs could be tied, and each space had its own bowl of water. Then we went in for our tea. It was there that I first met up with a "Bath bun," and I never want to have anything else.

Writing seems to elude me. There are days when I feel as if pursued by a demon. Where is my direction? I pray for a sign. Such great things I have held in thought for myself, and where am I on the road to any accomplishment? Then I think it is no demon but an angel with whom I am wrestling, and I will not let it go until it blesses me. I do seem to be standing still, not doing anything, not realizing the determination I started out with so boldly a few years ago.

In the Reading Room I kept returning to George Eliot as if my salvation were in her, and that led me to an American who wrote about the same time, Louisa May Alcott; that led me to Margaret Fuller and her counterpart in England, Harriet Martineau; that led me to Clara Barton and Florence Nightingale. Each one worked against the odds of convention and mores; each one was determined to make her life count, no matter what the cost. I filled a large notebook with my discoveries and comments about these six women. Perhaps this was the direction I had been praying for; perhaps my work lay not in creation but in interpretation. Talking about this with Bill, I felt a quiver of excitement way down inside me. I was possessed with an idea of biographies of nineteenth-century women on both sides of the Atlantic, women who began a foundation for twentieth-century thinking. The work was a challenge and, as I pursued my people through the stacks of the British Museum, I felt I had not eyes enough to read the books outlined for my study, nor hands enough to get onto paper the words that were flowing.

So I wrote, sometimes at the British Museum, sometimes in my room at Wythburn Court. I would be typing the pages soon. And then, perhaps, before the leaves began to fall from the great trees in the London parks, my leaves would be bundled into a box, to be sent across the Atlantic to Miss Louise Seaman.

A letter came from Loyola, "Two months without any word from you. That can mean only one thing."

May, 1931

"This is the day to go to Kew Gardens," Mrs. Balmain said one morning on the phone.

We agreed to meet at Victoria Station, with the dogs, and set forth in the afternoon. This is something I delighted in about England: dogs could go anywhere. At the station I bought their two tickets when I bought my own. On their leads they accompanied us into the compartment and behaved as they were expected to. Kew was beautiful. The day was sunny but cool, and the breezes were gentle. Green grass! Spring flowers! Swans going through a mating ritual! I was ecstatic with all that I was seeing.

"But wait," Mrs. Balmain said.

We walked on and approached a wooded area. I stood still. What had happened? Had the sky fallen through the budding beech trees and was it resting just above the ground? There was fragrance on the air, as exquisite as the sight that filled my eyes. Bluebells.

A path led right through them, and with the dogs close at heel we walked down it. What do you do when heaven lies at your feet in bell-like flowers on long, slender stems there in a wood as if they had just happened? Tea was being served outdoors at the pavilion, and we went there, but we talked little. A vision of sheer loveliness was in my mind, and Mrs. Balmain knew what seeing bluebells for the first time meant to me.

July, 1931

Summer in London is different from summer in America. I have worn a cotton dress exactly twice. Tweed skirts and wool jerseys are the rule, as they are through most of the year. However, they have always been my favorite clothes.

September, 1931

In Ireland I am whelmed with its beauty, and something else—a kind of leprechaun quality to life. Bill's Dublin manager, who sent us the wedding telegram about "a wee moose ne'er leaving your hoose" showed us everything. It began in Dublin, and, while Davey and Bill were talking business, I had time to explore the city, see the Book of Kells, watch swans on the Liffey, and adventure to my heart's content. When we went to Blarney Castle, Bill was the adventurer. I got in position to kiss the famous Stone. Davey and a guide held my ankles while I reached up to grasp the bar before they lowered me backward, all the time telling stories of how "they" did occasionally drop a person into the brambles below. I lost my nerve and begged them to pull me up, then they put Bill in position. He wasn't afraid. Perhaps I believed their stories and he didn't. Just as he kissed the Stone, I leaned over the parapet and got a picture of him.

Bill's camera is a part of all our journeys. He's getting more and more expert, using lenses and filters, and measuring the light with a meter. It's all very mathematical, and he has that kind of mind, so it fits together. Next to me, he says, his Leica is his dearest possession. Lakes of Killarney, thatched cottages, people, the village

24

of Adair are not only singing in memory but are captured in pictures to be relived whenever we want. Now it's Bantry Bay, a great sweep of the southwest coast cradling the Atlantic, a tiny town, and an inn that makes us feel we must be living in another time. Last night we went up to bed holding candles in our hands, in the morning we washed in china bowls, pouring the water from a huge pitcher. Right now I am sitting on a rock by the sea, with the Bay so calm it mirrors the sky, and church bells ringing in the distance. Bill is off with his camera, and I am bringing my notes up to date.

October, 1931

Friends had been coming into my life—not the casual kind, but the kind I knew were forever. Marguerite Puttick asked me to write a play for the children in her school, so I started on *The Golden Key*. This would be quite different from the biographies, but they were at a stage when it would be good to set them aside for a while and let them mellow. A play was new for me, but it was just another step in a writing career, and I intended to try every one that came my way.

November, 1931

I was alone when they came. It was Elsie's afternoon off and Bill was not back from the office. Twelve red roses. Oh, Bill! I took them, one by one, and placed them in a tall vase that showed their stems and gave support to the buds that would soon open. The dogs watched me, as they do everything. I wanted to laugh and cry with happiness, but what I did was sit on the floor by the fire, with a dog on each side, and watch the flames, and think. When Bill got home he had a package under his arm from Asprey's, with a note—

A softish cashmere rug, my dear,
For the nap you never take,
May it keep you warm and snug,
    my dear,
Should you doze off by mistake.

Year's End, *1931*

Two years ago, even a year ago, it seemed as if the life we were building together might go on in the same delightful way for a long time, but that was not to be. Events in the world were beginning to make inroads on our world. Mr. Walter Mangum, the president, hinted to Bill that the company might soon be sold, and, if so, Bill might want to start making other plans. But not yet, Mr. Mangum said, things may change for us all. The shafts of light before the sun goes down are long, often very bright, and not to be ignored. We would continue to live as we had, but we would prepare ourselves for a change. When we talked about that possibility, as we did so often, I used the word "ready" while Bill used the word "willing." There is a difference.

1932

A MOUNTAIN VIEW

Winter, 1932

These are trying times for Bill, with decisions to be made, plans to be adjusted. I want to help all I can, and that means giving him my undivided self. I won't lose my interest in the biographies, even though they must be set aside again, nor my impetus, for so much has already been done. Memory is like a little room on which I shut the door for a while, and there the biographies are safely waiting. Evening after evening we sit by the fire in our soft green room, talking. Rosy tulips make shadow shapes on the wall and gleam, reflected, in the polished mahogany of the sofa table. My hands are quietly occupied with my needlepoint. The dogs sleep, oblivious to the changes we are contemplating.

The business that Bill gave so much of himself to for many years had been sold. He was handsomely compensated in sterling, an amount sufficient to see us through a year or more of careful living. The company was being disbanded, the Mangums were returning to America. This did not happen in one day, but on the day that it was made final, we talked far into the night.

We decided to take a period of time to assess our life. Bill had worked hard for more than twenty years, and before turning to some other form of usefulness, he needed a long view, and what better place to have it than in the mountains? By the time we went to bed our decision was made. We would leave London with its grayness and its magic, Wythburn Court with its colorful comfort, the friends that had been slowly but surely made, and we would go to Switzerland.

"But, Bill, you've always been a businessman, an executive."

"Yes, since before I never went to college, but 'there's always a new firing line.' " Quoting one of his favorites, Justice Holmes, he brought our discussion to an end.

March 25, 1932

This stands out as one of the Great Days in our lives. It was an English Quarter Day, when rents are paid, but not for us. The flat was let, the furniture was put into storage, good-bys were said. We were off with the dogs and a miscellaneous collection of luggage to spend Easter Week in Paris, then we would be on our way to Switzerland.

April, 1932

We were wakened at the border by a customs official wanting to see our passports. He asked only one question and it was about the dogs: *"Quelle race?"* Searching my sleepy mind, I came out with the word, *"Écossais."* That seemed to satisfy him completely. Soon the train was on its way again and the gates of beauty opened to us.

At Montreux we found a pension that was near a

park where the dogs could run. In it there were bird boxes and trays for seeds and crumbs that carried signs Pensez aux oiseaux. The air was fresh off the waters of Lake Geneva and from the snow-covered heights of Mont Blanc and the mountains that were near and far. Each one challenged us, but we knew we had to find a place to live first. Every day we took the neat little train that wound its way up into the Bernese Oberland, and every day we got off at a village a little higher up to see if we could find something to rent for the summer. The fields were filled with narcissus, and children were gathering them in great armfuls. Three weeks went by, and I became impatient, but Bill assured me that a chalet existed and we would know it when we saw it.

So we did the day we reached Gstaad and breathed air like none other.

The estate agent in the village referred us to the local guide, Fritz Gempeler. He had built a chalet for himself and his wife to retire into someday but as yet it was not occupied. It was a mile up—everything was always up or down—from the village, and on the Turbach. "Go talk with him," the agent said.

Bill's German was better than my French, but both were needed, as Herr and Frau Gempeler knew no English. They lived in the village, but we were soon on the road with them to Heimeli. With more smiles than words the Gempelers showed the chalet to us. When we saw it, Bill and I simply looked at each other. It was small, snug, new, built into a hillside, with enough space for a terraced garden. From the balcony we saw a mighty line of mountains in which the Wildhorn was centered; in the narrow valley below the chalet, the Turbach ran, its waters adding music to the day. The rent was reasonable, the furnishings adequate, the dogs as delighted as we. In German that was improving by the minute, Bill told Fritz that we would like to have Heimeli until mid-October.

Fritz cared less about the arrangements than that he would be the one to guide us on the slopes as soon and as often as we wished. Perhaps it had taken three weeks, but time slid away in the wonder of Heimeli, and we could not wait to get back to Montreux, collect our belongings and move in. On our way back to Gstaad we stepped aside for some cows going up to high pasture. Their great bells, differing in size and tone, were more than a melodious symphony: to us they were a paean of thanksgiving.

May 20, 1932

The days in Heimeli are falling into a pattern of simple joy and satisfying work. Lotte, a German au pair girl whom we had known of in London, has come out to join us. She wants to learn English and do housework in return. In the mornings, in the small room that looks out upon vast mountains, I resume work on the biographies; Bill goes off with his camera; Lotte sings about her housework, starts turning earth for a garden, takes the dogs down to the Turbach. Afternoons we try our feet on the winding paths, little climbs preparing us for big ones. We bask in the glory of sunshine. Oh heaven, oh earth, oh God of both, what treasures are poured around us! Seeds are planted, sprouts appear, and in fields and meadows and along roadsides the pageant of wildflowers is enacted. It is a golden age.

June, 1932

Bill came back from the Saanen Market with a roll full of film that he is eager to have developed and a head full of things he wants to write. He has been working all afternoon on a story of Market Day, intermingling writing with laying a stone walk along our flower-vegetable garden. He wrote with the care and precision he applies to everything, then read his pages through to himself. Even before showing them to me, he tore them into bits. "You're the writer," he said, "I'll be the picture maker."

It takes courage to sit in judgment on yourself. I admired him and almost envied him, because I found it hard to destroy my work. That evening we had the first produce from our garden—turnip tops! Did anything ever taste better?

July, 1932

In this world of shining sun and shimmering mountains, there is rain at times; and there were dark days for Bill when a damp cloth over his eyes and quiet were the only remedy. He came out of every attack with his wonderful smile and more determination than ever to get the most from every good day, every new experience.

Friends from England and America were finding their way to us, and we were glad that, small as Heimeli was, we could make room for them. Visitors with whom we had great fun were the Hill children, whom we had grown to know well in England, as their parents were our good friends. Erskine was thirteen, Margaret was eleven, Barbara was eight. We did many small climbs during the week they were with us and their response to the heights—the joys and the dangers—matched their years.

One day, while we were having luncheon on the

balcony and looking toward the mountains, Lotte said, "Tonight the moon is full."

That was enough. Whoever wants to waste a full moon?

We laid our plans, packed rucksacks with necessities, and at five thirty started off. It was hot. We walked steadily, that pace learned from Fritz, up, up, until we reached the first point of the Durreschild two hours later and just as a twilight glow was turning to orange behind the distant rim of mountains. We found a sheltered spot near a rock, gathered sticks and made a fire. We had supper, big bowls of Maggi soup, fresh bread, and fruit, and waited for the moon to rise. The dogs were excited, but never ventured beyond the rim of light cast by the fire; the children were spellbound. I had my beloved anthology, *The Gypsy Trail,* in my sack, and we read aloud in the flickering light. Lotte read some of the German poems, translating as she read; I let William Blake speak for us all—

> The moon, like a flower
> In heaven's high bower,
> With silent delight
> Sits and smiles on the night.

A glow began to spread across the sky to the east, then the moon appeared slowly, oh so slowly, washing the valley with silver, lighting up the distant peaks. Barbara whispered

> Slowly, silently, now the moon
> Walks the earth in her silver shoon.

By midnight it was bright enough to show the downward way. The fire was out. The rucksacks almost empty. We went singing over the path and reached

Heimeli an hour later, filled with beauty. "I shall never forget this as long as I live," said Barbara as I tucked her into bed.

August 10, 1932

Fritz feels we are in condition for the Rubli, and that is a real climb, an almost vertical slab of rock towering above the valley. Looking at it has thrilled me and sent a shudder through me at the same time.

August, 1932

We left Heimeli at 3:30 A.M.—no dogs this time, but Frau Gempeler was coming in during the day to see to them. A half hour later we met Fritz on the path to the Rubli. All was hushed and still, the dark just paling into dawn as we set off. Fritz led with that even mountain pace, not fast, not slow, that will carry one for a day if need be. Through the glories of the sunrise we went, up, up, past the last alp and the Rubli hut to the base of the ascent. There Fritz uncoiled the rope he had carried over his shoulders and tied us onto it. Our rucksacks were left in a heap, only the leader had his, and that was Fritz. His eyes ran down each one of us to be sure there was nothing loose—no button undone, no shoe unlaced. He would be in the lead, Lotte and I in the middle, Bill at the end of the rope. The smile that was as much a part of Fritz as his sun-bronzed, wind-toughened countenance had disappeared. He was serious. His lively talk had come down to two words, *"Courage. Prenez garde."* Then we were off and up the sheer wall of rock.

We moved with caution, getting holds with

fingers, then gaining footholds with the tips of our boots, aware of a pull on the rope only if one of us slackened, yet always aware that in the rope was our safety, not as one, but as a team. It was 8 A.M. when we gained the summit and, suddenly, there was nothing higher.

A thrilling panorama was spread around us—green valleys, little villages, fields where cattle grazed, square-set hay barns, chalets whose small windows blinked under the jutting brows of their great roofs, and all rimmed by distant mountains whose white snows glistened in the sunshine. Fritz beamed at us all as if we had done some great thing, then he shook hands with us and said, "Bravo."

Still on the rope, but with slack between us, we stretched out on the rocks. Fritz opened his rucksack, filled cups with coffee still steaming from the thermos, unwrapped and offered us rolls that were crisp and crunchy. Two hours was the limit of our time, as the Rubli wall would become too hot for the needed holds. Lotte and I flattened out and breathed deeply. Bill wriggled around a boulder and lowered himself to the length of his portion of rope. When he came back he had in his teeth a bunch of edelweiss, which he gave to me. *"Comme le vrai amant!"* Fritz exclaimed. Rope holds were checked carefully before we started down. The descent was more difficult and hazardous than the ascent.

By noon we reached an open meadow where a spring bubbled into a hollowed log, a drinking trough for cows. Near it Fritz built a small fire of sticks, and soon the contents of another rucksack were emptied and he was frying bacon and eggs, buttering slabs of bread, and making coffee. Dessert was a tin of raspberries, the Hero brand, turned into our tin plates which had been mopped clean with bread. Full, happy, and feeling like conquerors, we stretched back on the turf. Cowbells could be heard in the distance, the sun was warm, the breeze off distant peaks was cool.

Turning around suddenly, I dislodged my rucksack and it started down the slope, bouncing and gaining speed. Fritz saw it and raced after it. Passing it, he reached out for it and it came bounding into his arms. He laughed, shrugged his shoulders, and when he handed it back to me it was almost the way Bill had handed me the edelweiss. Fritz had taught me that if something gets away from you, don't try to catch up with it, get ahead of it, outwit it, and let it come into your outstretched hands.

It was late in the afternoon when we finally reached Heimeli. Tired, yes, but so proud of our conquest that exhilaration made a mockery of fatigue.

August 28, 1932

This is an important day in my life. I have finished the biographies. The title Challenge *was inevitable—what it was to me when I started thinking about it during those long hours in the British Museum, what I hope the lives will be to every girl who reads them. I packed the typed pages in a box and wrapped them securely, addressed it to go* By Fast Ship, *then Bill and I ran all the way down to the village to get the package in the Post. Joy and relief for both of us, followed by rolls and coffee at the Bernerhof.*

"This calls for celebration," Bill said, and the kind we are taking is a bit of vagrancy.

Leaving Lotte to care for Heimeli and the dogs, we took off by train for two weeks of sheer adventure. Zurich, Lindau, Munich, Salzburg, Innsbruck, Garmisch, Lucerne, all revealed their charm to us. My notebook was crammed. Bill did many pictures.

We waited on the weather to climb the Wildhorn. Fritz had to be assured of two perfect days, and this was a time of year when change is in the air; but the right moment came. Bill, Lotte, and I with our gear in good shape set out with Fritz, taking the train to Lenk. Then we were off and up, walking slowly, climbing all the way, and the last part wearily. We trudged through the snow around the Iffigensee and Bill got a picture of the last rays of sun drawing a band of pure silver over the black water. It was twilight when we reached the Wildhorn hut, a low stone building with green-and-white angle-striped shutters. Inside was a great fireplace, a spring for water, and bunks built against the walls. The hut is a radial point for many mountains and other climbers were there, with different languages vibrating on the air. Food and rest was the order. After a meal that Fritz cooked, we stretched out on the boards of the bunks. Fritz said he would waken us with the first light. The only book I had tucked in my rucksack was our small *Runner's Bible,* but there was no light to read by. We wrote our names in the hut book and stamped our bible with C.A.S. Section Moleson Cabane Wildhorn 2315 meters, and the date.

By 6 A.M. we were on our way, climbing over a rough rocky area through a crimson and gold sunrise onto the glacier. The snow was deep and crusty, and Fritz had us on the rope. He went first, testing every foot of the way with his pickax, pointing to crevasses whose ice-blue walls made the air colder there than that around us. Going ever more slowly and cautiously, he looked back now and then and mouthed the word *"Courage."* If he said it, the wind took all sound away. It seemed interminable, the plodding through snow-fields. There was no stopping to rest. The wind was cruel and it forced us on. Then we gained the domed summit: 3264 meters! On one side was the long chain of the Alps, snow-covered, crevassed, glacier strewn, from Mont Blanc in France to the tips of the Dolomites in Austria; on the other, the sweep down into the green valleys of the Oberland.

It was worth everything to stand for those few thrilling moments on a crest of the world. Fritz shook hands with us all in turn. "Bravo," he said. "Bravo," he smiled. Then, swinging off his rucksack, he took out the thermos, handed cups to us, and filled them. The tea was steaming when it was poured, but lukewarm when it touched lips. The wind and the cold would not let us stay, nor would Fritz. It was imperative to get across the glacier field before the sun started melting the snow. *"Courage,"* he said as he checked the rope that linked us all.

This time Bill was in the lead, following the footsteps made earlier. The man at the end had more power to hold back if one of us made a misstep. It was high noon when we reached the hut. Fritz made bowls of soup while Bill changed the film in his camera, and soon we were off again, down, down the long kilometers to Lenk. Much of the way was through a bleak area of rock and snow. We saw five chamois, nimble and graceful. We stood still and watched them, scarcely breathing with the wonder, then one by one they trotted up a slope, stood for an instant on the horizon's rim silhouetted against a clear blue sky, and long enough for Bill to catch them on film, then dropped from sight. We walked on through a narrow pass and at last came into green fields where cattle grazed and children played. That night, when we looked on the Wildhorn from Heimeli's balcony, one thought was in our minds, "We have stood where clouds are resting."

September 28, 1932

Today a letter came from Miss Seaman—fast ship has served us well. "It is an interesting idea . . . shows careful research and the writing is thoughtful . . . but you are speaking through these people. When are you going to speak for yourself? I am returning Challenge as it is not for us. Your International Money Order more than covered the postage, so I am including one of our new books." She added a P.S. "Harvester is doing very well. The reviews have been consistently good and the sales are pleasing us and your brother."

Do I have the courage to do what Bill did with his piece on Saanen Market? No. Because I think the material may be useful sometime, in some way. It's just another challenge, but this time without a capital C.

October, 1932

And now the summer was memory; but living close to great mountains did something for us both. We said good-by to Heimeli and the Gempelers, to Lotte, who was returning to Germany, and to Sinna. A sudden illness just a week before snuffed out that stalwart life;

38

loyal comrade of my lonely years, dear companion during years of bliss. We placed his brave little body in the earth near where our garden had been, and Lotte said, "There is something of you which will always be a part of Switzerland." With Bara beside us and our luggage around us, we took the train down through the Bernese Oberland on a day of gently falling rain. The countryside was a tapestry of color, but the mountains were veiled.

We arrived in Paris as the sun, swimming out of a coral haze, touched the Seine bridges and the towers of Notre Dame with color. Soon we were installed in a charming flat in Passy loaned to us by some friends. Now I had the fun of keeping house in French for a while. Paris was unutterably beautiful. Leaves were falling and slim dark arms of trees were etched against misty vistas. It seemed noisy and rushing as I remembered the restraint in England, the politeness of Switzerland; but it was not for long. A return to America was imminent. We would sail in December, but before that I planned to return to England to make some arrangements, and Bill was to spend that time at an eye clinic where a specialist would help him if anyone could.

December, 1932

Out of Southampton, the channel was rough, but the S.S. *Franconia* took it steadily; and there was Bill on the dock at Cherbourg with other passengers waiting to be picked up. He was easily distinguished by the small black dog standing alertly beside him in the late light of afternoon. Two weeks had been too long and there was so much to talk about. Soon we were in our cabin,

Bara too, as this was an English ship. The steward brought tea, and time was before us.

"How was it to be back in England?"

"Oh, Bill, it was going home. The train seemed to be hurrying on its way from Dover to London, and it was almost too dark to see anything, but tea was served and the soft voices were like music. That sense of unchangeableness always sturdies me."

"And did you get everything done?"

"Yes, and I saw so many of our friends, went to the theater, did some shopping. But you?"

Bill was silent, then he smiled. "I have sight. I shall use it while I have it."

"An operation? Did he think that would help?"

Bill shook his head almost imperceptibly. "Only when the pain becomes too great, but that won't be for a long time. Five years or more." Bill said it as if five years might be forever.

There was so much more to talk about, and while the ship floundered its way through heavy seas we made our plans. Sometimes it seemed that we were always making plans with spaces between when we lived the plans.

"That's the best part of life," Bill said, "always looking ahead, but living in the present."

1933–1935

AMERICAN INTERLUDE

It has been an interlude, a time between, and we have returned to England, settling in as if we had never left. Facing the present fact of our lives, we know that our tastes are simple, our needs few, and that we can make what we have go much farther in England; and we can live at our own pace.

In America there was so much noise and hurry, so much advertising, so much clamoring for attention, and everything was so efficient. But I relished the easy friendliness and the spontaneity. The air sparkled, the sky was so often cloudless, the buildings pointed up and up. Yet, during our first months, the times were trying. It was the depth of the depression. The February day when the banks closed and President Roosevelt spoke to the nation on the radio, people listened anxiously. There was need for a leader to give heart to the country. His words "The only thing we have to fear is fear itself" spoke to us all.

We saw friends and visited families, then we settled in Boston for a while and began making contacts. One led to another. Bill's photographs with my text to accompany them found their places in newspapers, many in the *Christian Science Monitor*. Checks, small though they were, began to come with delightful regularity. Bill followed every lead he could to make a business connection. There were few openings in those days, and none for a man whose sight was limited. This in itself proved to work for him, as his life insurance policy carried a disability clause that could be invoked, relieving him of paying further premiums and entitling him to a monthly check. It was not large, but it could be counted on.

A friend loaned us her car whenever we wanted it, and we made frequent trips throughout New England, staying in old towns, walking the country roads, wondering when—we had dropped the "if"—we would see the perfect place and our dream of a little farm would come true. But, for now, the signs pointed to England. Miss Clements wrote that she had produced two of the plays I had written for Miss Puttick's School and when would I be back to write another? Bertha Miller of *The Horn Book Magazine* suggested articles she would like that could be done only in England. The *Monitor* was ready to schedule a series of interviews with outstanding English individuals; they would continue the illustrated travel essays, and welcome any book reviewing.

One night, adding everything up and considering what England meant to us, we made the decision to return. And at the thought, the windows of heaven seemed to open for us.

We were only on the edge of accomplishment in our separate but often combined fields of writing and picture making. We knew it would be some time before we were really established, but we felt we could make our way more easily in the gentle clime of England. The pace was too swift in America, the pressures too many.

It meant a shift, not an uprooting, as we had never put down roots; it would mean quarantine for Bara; but, as far as we could see, it was the better way for a time.

Before we left, we borrowed our friend's car and went up into southern New Hampshire, spending nights in little inns that had history to them, discovering towns that charmed us—Hancock, Peterborough, Francestown, Temple. We spent a day on the big mountain that dominated the countryside—Monadnock—and saw from its height forests and lakes and rivers, clearings and villages. Bill took pictures of old houses and tall church spires, animals, trees, people. "Nothing particular," he said again and again. "Just the way the country is. I want to be able to see it when we're on the other side of the ocean. Remembering may be the sometime magnet."

On the ship that took us back to England, I read one of Mary Ellen Chase's very New England books, *Mary Peters*. A certain passage seemed to be for us, and I read it to Bill:

> Her life that afternoon had been rounded into a perfect circle, complete and fulfilled. She had nothing to regret, everything to remember with gratitude. Most people were wrong about life, she thought. It was not a struggle against temptation as she had been taught in church. Nor was it a search for truth as the philosophers said, or even for happiness, much as humanity craved happiness. It was rather a kind of waiting—a waiting upon the graciousness and the bounty of the things which had been, in order that the things to come might find one free and unafraid.

Bill said, "We've made another circle. Now, to see what the next will be. Didn't Emerson have something to say about circles?"

"Indeed he did, and that essay is one of the most marked in my book." I reached far back into memory and found a few words: "Something about man's life being a self-revolving circle, small at first, then growing larger, always expanding. That's the thought."

What did I notice as the S.S. *Samaria* steamed into Southampton Water—the softness in the light and in the air, and moments later in the voices of the people. There seemed to be no clamor or stress. On the train to London I looked out on a countryside that was still green, with the muted colors of autumn just visible. Everything was neat, and there were flowers blooming in the little gardens of cottages along the way. Then it was London, with twilight coming down like a cloak and that feeling of quiet stability. There were no raucous horns or hurrying crowds, but the gray of buildings, the red of buses; and in Victoria Station friends to welcome us.

"In returning and rest shall ye be saved." We have come back to England to accomplish something. As we establish ourselves in our work, we will be making ourselves ready for the next circle.

1936
LONG LIVE THE KING

January, 1936

"The King is dead! Long live the King!"

King George has died after a long illness, and there is mourning throughout the land. Even I wear a black armband on the left sleeve of my coat. But within moments his son, Edward VIII, was proclaimed king, so England is not without a monarch.

As the funeral procession passed on its way to Westminster Abbey, Bill and I stood in a huge crowd on the edge of Hyde Park. People all around us were snapping pictures of the cortege, the horses, the soldiers. Bill took a picture of the crowd, focusing on two men just ahead of us—one was very tall with a silk top hat, squared shoulders, every inch of him a lord or a duke; the other, a shabby little man, his cap pulled down over his ears and his hair straggling on his collar.

"Nothing in particular," Bill said, but when it was printed, he entered it in a competition the *Daily Express* was holding. They thought it was something in particular, illustrating "the power of the throne to bring all classes together." It won first prize, was printed on the

45

front page, and wherever the *Daily Express* was read and sold Bill's picture was seen.

High Summer, 1936

What wonderful things happen! Bill learned of a house we could rent in Kent in a village named Trottis-cliffe; after the damp cold winter in London, it was alluring. We knew the charm of an English spring; here was a chance to live in and into the unfolding year.

So we took White House for six months. The rent was low, because the owners were to be away and wanted to have the place cared for just as it was, with a maid, a gardener, and a cat. White House had a history going back five hundred years, but only its recent years were known about. Joseph Conrad had lived in it and here he wrote his novel *Victory*. There was a picture of him leaning from a window and calling to his wife in the garden. Sir Philip Gibbs had lived in it. It must be a good place for a writer. The rooms are all small, as once it was three little shops, but the garden is large.

The April night we arrived, Nelly had coal fires burning brightly in the tiny sitting room and in our bedroom. She soon produced a massive tea "to cheer you." I've got used to being called "madam," and I like to hear Bill referred to as "the master." The cat resented Bara at first and then made up to him seductively; gentleman that Bara is, he tolerated either mood.

Back of the house there was a deep and lovely garden, protected on one side by a gray wall, on the other by a beech hedge. The garden was bright with daffodils when we arrived, and there were primroses everywhere. The earth was alight with them; they were peeking out of hedgerows, blooming in unlikely places. Looking from the house up the village street, we could see two oasthouses, a flintstone church with a duck pond close by, the one store—once called the Universal Provider and now known as the Little Wonder—a few houses, their tiled roofs mossy and mellow, and a triangular Green. Beyond are the North Downs, flinging a protective arm across the countryside. This is the way the pilgrims walked to Canterbury, which is not far distant.

It was cold, at first, and there were some light dustings of snow, but by the end of April, warmth came and with it leaves appeared and birds arrived, their chatter a background to our days.

I couldn't get away from the feeling that I was living in a storybook, for things happened just the way I've read about them. The vicar and his sister came to call, and of course Nelly had tea ready. . . . Two men appeared with a basket, saying they were taking an egg collection for the Maidstone Hospital and they hoped to get hundreds. We found six in the larder that Nelly said she could spare. . . . The butcher in West Malling did not mind bringing the fish, as the fishmonger does not come as far as Trosley—that's the way the village name is pronounced here. And he would accommodate the greengrocer, too. . . . My shoes, needing new soles and left at the cobbler a mile away, were delivered by the newspaper boy on his morning round.

Progress had arrived in the shape of electricity, which never got farther than tarred poles left on the Green. "With the sun giving so many hours of light, we'll not want to be connected until end of summer." Very sensible we think, for the lamplit house satisfies. Another evidence of progress was the large bright TCB pillar-box that almost dwarfed the Little Wonder. "It's taking wonderfully," the villagers said. It was a new model, one of the first to be set up anywhere. "And they put it in Trosley! That shows what they think of us."

The walks were lovely in any direction, but especially up on the Downs, where it was high and windy. I went off with my notebook, Bill with his camera. He came back with film to be developed, I with more flowers than I could name. On the Downs one morning I stopped and caught my breath—bluebells! The ground was azure with their bloom. When I first heard the cuckoo, I thought it was in my dreams; but Bill woke me and said "It's true—" So we went for an early walk, and we heard the call across the fields as flight took him. I thought of the old rhyme "—he comes in May, In June he changes his tune, In July he prepares to fly, In August go he must." Blossoms and leaves were fairly leaping into being and the countryside was different each day than it was the day before. The sun was so warm that Nelly had breakfast for us in the garden. Birds were busy all around us.

"It's like living in an aviary," Bill said, "a tapestry of sound."

It was like the needlepoint chair seats I was making, with their birds and their flowers.

Such loveliness! Everything that can blossom blossomed. The beech hedge was softly green, pear and cherry blossoms were pink and white overhead, while bees droned in them and apple blossoms drifted down the wind. Lilacs poured their fragrance. Edward brought the kitchen garden to the table—cress, rhubarb, lettuce, radish. "And there'll be more, all summer there'll be more."

Friends from London, even from America, came to visit us, and we led them on scented walks along the Pilgrim's Way, past the Coldrum Stones, that strange circle that is a relic of primitive man. At night we went to the Downs to hear the nightingale. But White House was a place for work, too. I resisted the temptation to be outside all the time and settled myself at a plain table in the little room that looks up the village street. I was writing short essays to fit Bill's pictures, and every week one went on its way across the ocean. The new pillar-box was just the right size for mailing the envelopes.

One sunny day led to another into the high tide of summer. Lilies now stood tall in the border along the gray wall, with delphinium and roses and lavender. Fruit was ripening. Of all the people who came to stay a few days or a week, the most welcome were Bob and his Martha on their honeymoon. They came when we were picking cherries and drying lavender. Bob was a man of business by then. He was pleased to talk about his book, but nothing would induce him to write another.

"You're the writer in the family," he said with that wonderful smile that always made everything all right.

He was puzzled about what we were doing, or not doing. He liked the house and the garden, the quaintness of the village, the beauty of the countryside, the comfort of having servants. "But what are you doing except having a good time?"

The explanation was too long to make on a radiant day, with flowers and their fragrance around us, birds and their singing. The simplest thing was to tell him that we were establishing ourselves in a new way.

"But you won't be here after the summer, will you?"

"No, we'll be back in London."

"What doing?"

"What we're doing here—writing, making pictures. Being."

Then we dropped the subject. The day was too nice, he was too happy; but in that brief encounter of words, a national difference became clear to me—in America one must be *doing,* in England *being* seemed to have a reason.

Writing mornings, walking afternoons, reading evenings, so the days went by with a modicum of work in house and garden, as Nelly and Edward had their charges. We knew, too, that we would have gone down in their estimation had we done work not fitting for "the gentry." Sometimes I chafed at the restriction, but we were in England and that was the way. "It may not ever be so," Bill said, the gentleness in his tone, like Bob's smile, closing the matter softly.

Some friends made in books are forever. Before I was ten I had read George MacDonald's books. *At the Back of the North Wind* I have read many times, always finding something more in it to stir my thought. This summer I was deep in his novels, especially *Sir Gibbie* and *Donal Grant.* But, much as I longed to read *Sir Gibbie* aloud to Bill, I could not cope with the Scottish dialect. My eyes slid over what my tongue could not twist itself around. I read MacDonald's life, a big rewarding book, and it made me feel wonderfully close to him.

When Marguerite came down to visit us, she brought with her the three volumes of his poetry, out of print for many years. For the most part they were long, didactic, and very Victorian, but jewels were among them and these I could read aloud to Bill and Marguerite as we sat in the garden. Way deep in me something began to stir. How could I bring this aspect of MacDonald to people again—not the storyteller still so well known, or the preacher so long forgotten, but the poet?

"I know his youngest daughter, Winifred, Lady Troup," Marguerite said. "When you get back to London, I'd like you two to meet. She lives in Kensington."

There was a week when we had no visitors. Nelly tiptoed about the house, and even Edward ceased his whistling when he came in with vegetables from the garden. Bara would not leave Bill's darkened room except when I insisted. The attack was one of the shortest, and my heart leaped with hope that perhaps we were winning the battle; but when Bill returned to his camera, he asked me to read the fine print on his light meter.

The Hill children, Erskine, Margaret, and Barbara, came to visit. Three years had not made too much change in them, and this was something that delighted us. In England children seemed to remain children so much longer. We had noticed the way they shot up with such rapidity in America, as if impatient to get on with life. Barbara was still the adventurer, but becoming more careful about spending money. The day we went to visit Knole House, Bill gave her tuppence for the ladies' room. When she returned, "It wasn't worth it," she announced with scorn that would have pleased her Scottish father.

One afternoon, while Erskine was up on a ladder helping Edward gather early apples and Margaret and I were stripping lavender from its stalks, Bill told Barbara a story. It was such a good story that I thought he must be reading it, but he wasn't. It was coming straight from that fertile mind of his. Later I asked if I could type it and send it to a publisher. He demurred and twitted me about my indefatigable optimism. However, I did type it as I had heard him tell it, and when I read to him *The Frog, the Penny and the Big Black Tree,* he laughed at his own words. Frederick Warne and Company, who had published the Beatrix Potter books, seemed a logical place to send it, so it went to them with postage enclosed for return.

Late Summer, 1936

The days, so long in late June that it was light at ten o'clock, were shortening noticeably. In the flower garden the colors now were the purple of Michaelmas daisies and the burnished gold of chrysanthemums; the vegetables that Edward brought in for the table were cabbages and brussels sprouts. Our lease was up in September. In April it had seemed impossible to think of ever leaving White House. Now it was becoming quite possible to yearn for London.

The day we went into the Little Wonder to say good-by, the postmistress handed me a long, thin envelope. "That's one you'll like," she said. She knew the difference in weight, and the meaning of a self-addressed envelope. She was right. It was an acceptance of one of my essays, and it held a check. I opened it and peeked in just for the fun of telling her that what she surmised was true. She smiled and handed Bill a small square envelope with a London postmark. We waited until we got back to White House to read it. Bill couldn't believe what it said, but I could: "We received your story and would like to consider publishing it

52

with illustrations by Mr. Cyrus Hall. Will you come up to London sometime soon to discuss arrangements?"

With one leap, Bill had become a book writer. Now there was every reason to return to London.

October, 1936

The flat at Edwardes Square is small, but it seems good to be surrounded by our own things again—especially our books. The Square itself is our joy. All who live on it have a key for entrance into it—the greenest of lawns, the richest of shrubbery, and the neatest of pebbled paths. Though we are in the heart of Kensington and embraced by London, there are still birds around us, and the clop of hooves as the milkman makes his early rounds, his small horse always knowing exactly where to stop and when to go on.

Marguerite took me to call on Lady Troup, and I felt as if I had yet another friend for life. I think she felt that way too, for it was so easy for us to talk about her father and of what I wanted to do in making a selection of his poems for publication. She said that she would help me, and I knew that I could turn to her. A small and charming person, she had the fragility of age, but the strength that I had found in her father's books.

Bill was busy with "his publishers." How thrilling that sounded! As soon as he went to call on the firm of Frederick Warne, he was informed that the artist had already done the illustrations, that the book would be published in the spring, and did he have another story in mind? "Yes, indeed," Bill said with certainty.

We were never at a loss for children, either those of friends, or those in Marguerite Puttick's School, or those who rolled their hoops or trundled their tricycles on the paths of the Square. Bill had only to take his key, turn it in the iron gate and start into the Square, with

53

Bara beside him, to be surrounded by an assortment of children, happily leaving their nannies for the man with a story to tell. *Dennis the Donkey* grew as much with the help of the children as through Bill's imagination. The firm of Warne was delighted and even improved on the first contract.

These were productive days for me. I was working on a series of stories about a certain Scottish terrier named Kilts, based on Bara's adventures, of course. The *Monitor* took every one I sent. I embarked on the interviews, and somehow it never occurred to me to feel nervous in the presence of Sybil Thorndike, or Elisabeth Bergner, or Vera Brittain, or any others. Before meeting with each one, I found out as much as was available. I knew what questions I wanted to ask. I listened when they talked to me, taking only a few notes in a shorthand of my own.

As often as possible, we saved our weekends for walking. We had a special day of sun and wind in the Chilterns. With our inch-to-a-mile Ordnance Survey map, our rucksacks, and Bara trotting happily beside us, we followed a wide green track that wound slowly up Ivinghoe Beacon. Its top is not a thousand feet, but once gained, there was nothing between us and the sky. Spur after spur of beech-covered hills disappeared into the distance, while near us were box trees and waist-high bracken. We came upon a signpost:

NORTH POLE	2760 MILES
LONDON	44 MILES
STAR TOP'S END	1 MILE

We chose the one that sounded as if it might be the farthest but was the nearest and came to a small hamlet. There was an inn, once an old house, set in a velvet lawn, lattice windows thrusting ivy aside. Inquiring if we might have tea, we were told we could, in the garden; so we went through a paneled room with sun shining on polished oak and silver to the garden. There were a few leaves falling, a few birds chittering, and soon a tea appeared that was all a high tea should be —hot scones and thin slices of buttered bread, eggs in cups, honey and jam, and a great pot of tea under a tea cozy to keep it warm. We were well fortified for the five-mile walk back to Beaconsfield and the train to London. This is the sort of day I shall always remember, essence of the England we knew and loved.

December 6, 1936

The year always begins to close and open again with my birthday. This year is more than ever special, as so much is opening for both of us. It begins to seem that the plowing and seeding we've done for so long, the watering and weeding, are producing grain. Reaping time is near.

Year's End, 1936

For the past seven years I've kept account of work sent out, marking acceptances and their amounts. Up to this year the acceptances have been few and the amounts small, but now the entries in both left and right columns of my little ledger are looking quite respectable.

1937

HIGH HOLIDAY

February, 1937

Audrey and I were having tea at Fortnum and
Mason's. We always had much to talk about to catch
each other up on.

"You've been busy?"

"Oh, yes, articles and essays, book reviews, some
interviews," I enumerated, "plays for a school."

"But you're not going to do that kind of piecework
forever?"

It was hard to find words to answer her. "I haven't
yet found—" I started, fumbling.

She cut me short. "Isn't there some one thing that
you know just a little more about than anyone else?
Write that."

She didn't give me time to disagree, to object, but
went on talking about a play she had seen the night
before, and we never got back to the subject of me.

On the bus from Piccadilly to Kensington, her
question returned to me and my inner answer was, "Of
course not. I've led a very usual sort of life, nothing
spectacular has ever happened to me." Arguments

came to me, but her words were persistent, and the wheels of the bus picked them up, droning ". . . something you know . . . more about . . . than anyone else." Ridiculous, I answered the droning. Then something took hold of me. In Switzerland, I had seen the way three children, different in age and temperament, reacted to the high mountains, to the challenge of climbing, to danger, to beauty. And with that memory I was off. My whole being was quivering. But how to make it into a story?

At supper I told Bill I had an idea for a book. I couldn't say much more, for I have learned that an idea calling to be written must not be spent in spoken words.

"Think on," he said.

And I did—walking with Bara in Kensington Gardens, sitting at my desk and looking at the plane tree outside the window. Whatever I was doing, the idea was there in the back of my mind, growing; and there were pages on my desk with writing on them that proved something was happening.

June, 1937

Once I had found the way to make it into a story —Michael and Meredith Lamb going out to Switzerland with their Uncle Tony—it had started. It grew as the leaves on the plane tree, from an inner surge. The people became real. The background was there in the experiences we had had, all jotted down in those little notebooks I had carried around with me; the stage for the action was in the pictures Bill had taken. Every time I wanted to be in Switzerland, I could be there by looking at his album. The work went fast, but when summer drew near, I was ready to put all those hand-written pages aside and plan with Bill a holiday on the Isle of Skye.

July, 1937

Grace Allen, whom we had known in America, now married and living in London, was with the Oxford University Press. They were doing a new edition of W. W. Tarn's *The Treasure of the Isle of Mist,* and they wanted Bill to do pictures for it. Phyllis, our delightful and dependable daily, would take care of Bara and the flat. We would have three whole weeks Skye-larking!

Bill was making a name for himself. His picture of Iffigensee, the lake near the Wildhorn hut, had won first prize in a photographic exhibition; and his George V picture had been widely seen. Of the comments he was receiving, the one that pleased him most was that "William McGreal, relying on the richness of black and white, can do more than many who depend on color." Bertha Miller, writing from Boston, was glad that the Tarn book was to come back after being out of print for some years. She told us what Anne Carroll Moore had to say about it: "There is a windswept fantasy of youth and autumn which I always reread in September. When I begin to find books of the year lacking in strength of background, in appeal to the imagination, in skill in the choice of words, I turn to *The Treasure of the Isle of Mist.*"

Grace warned us that she could give us no clear directions, for when the distinguished scholar wrote *The Treasure* as a fairy tale for his daughter, he had purposefully disguised place-names. We would have to go in the spirit of detectives, tracking down every clue and hoping to come upon those that would lead us rightly. I read the book aloud to Bill, and he made a list of places in the text that called for illustration—the Atlantic half asleep, the great West cave, the big house, the fairy bridge, a pale dawn coming up out of the sea, the jagged gray range of the Cuchullins, and many more. We would be off with an Ordnance Survey Map, plenty of film, stout shoes, clothes that would take any weather and a copy of Samuel Johnson's *A Journey to the Western Islands of Scotland.*

August, 1937

We left London in the evening of an extremely hot day, with a third-class compartment all to ourselves. The wonder of visiting a land new to us and yet so near beggared sleep. The first glimpse from the window the next morning was of wild moors, craggy mountains, dark rivers, tiny burns, and purple patches of heather. The country grew more dramatic as we approached the fishing town of Mallaig, where we took the boat to Skye. Rain came on, but it did not hide the dim majestic line of the Coolins (properly spelled Cuchullins, but I'm spelling it the way the people pronounce it) nor the green lushness of the fields.

It was late afternoon when we reached Portree, a protected harbor and a gray stone village with all its life at that moment centering at the quay. There were lean-faced lads in kilts, bright-cheeked girls, bearded men, women hugging black shawls about their shoulders, and dogs. Broad Scots was in the air, and the skirl of bagpipes to set my blood racing. The sun was shining, but clouds thick and black gathered, and rain fell again, veiling the distant mountains. When next the sun appeared, it was with a rainbow thrown from the thatch of a small cottage to a boat in the harbor.

The weather that first afternoon gave us a hint of what to expect, and I realized what Dr. Johnson meant when he said those islands were often "incommoded by very frequent rains." Such swift changes and shifts of wind created cloud formations that thrilled Bill. Using his light meter and different lenses and filters, he could make sunlight look like moonshine and get whatever effects he wanted.

Our lodgings overlooked the harbor, and the welcome was typical. "If you wait a wee moment, I'll have tea for you."

We went to our room and, while I was unpacking, Bill discovered "the necessary," He came back to tell me of the sign that hung near—BATHS BY ARRANGEMENT. LIGHTS OUT AT 11 P.M.

Early the next morning we were off on our search. We walked along the harbor, scrambled up the steep hillside to Fingal's Seat, sheltered under a rock with a huddle of sheep during a bout of rain, tramped across a moor with the sun turning it into a purple sea. Skye is a land of eerie enchantment, of wild, weird beauty. Every rock seems to imprison legend, everyone seems to believe in the "wee folk," and every other person has the second sight. It is like no other place in the world, I am sure—bleak and barren, often shrouded with mist. When the sun shines, dazzling colors are revealed, and there is a splendor to the blue sky with its magnificent cloud formations. "It fairs up quickly," we were told, and so we discovered.

Looking always for the clue that would lead us to the site of *The Treasure,* we went by bus to the northern end of the island. We stopped at a small building that said Home Industries, and Bill bought me a Skye-blue scarf. Duntulum Castle was a ruin, but near it was a corrugated tin shack with a sign "Ian Stewart, Tailor." "And that's where I'd like to have a suit made," Bill said. We saw cattle with curved horns and shaggy hair, and we passed many flocks of sheep, three hundred in one flock, our driver said. He stopped the bus until they had gone by, the dogs alert and conscientious, the shepherds leisurely.

Another day we went in a southerly direction. At Sligachan we left the bus and took the path to Glen Brittle. It was rocky, uphill, with the jagged Coolins piercing the sky behind us. Bill took many pictures, knowing they might be useful sometime. A fine mist was in the air, scarcely to be felt until the wind blew it against our faces. At the top of the pass, the view down the Glen was of a great bare scooped-out hollow, with a river winding its way to the sea. It was stark and lonely; we seemed the only evidence of life until three deer came cautiously over a ledge near where we stood. We looked at each other. They were the first to move, but not in flight, simply because it was time to go.

We felt sure now that what we were seeking must be on the west coast. Before leaving Portree we wanted to call on Old Donal, who, we had heard, had the second sight. Grace had warned us not to say anything about the purpose of our visit to anyone, lest word get back to Mr. Tarn.

"You'll find Donal's shieling just a wee walk up the Struan Road," our landlady said.

I wondered just how far "wee" was, for I was learning about understatement. Only the night before I had been describing something to one of our fellow lodgers and was met with the comment: "Would you not think you might be a bit overrating?" And I was learning about time-talking. More than once I had asked a question and thought I had not been heard, for nothing seemed to happen; but the answer came, in time, and always in the soft voice of the Gael, which was music to my ears.

The sun was strong and warm, the breeze full, and most of the morning gone, when we saw the shieling we knew must be Old Donal's. He was in a nearby bog, tossing peat.

"Are you Donal?" Bill asked.

"There's more than one Donal hereabouts, which one are you seeking?"

"The one who has the second sight."

"Ah well," and there was a smile on his face, "there are those who say I have the gift." So he heaved the sack of peat to his shoulder and led us to the shieling, telling us of it the while.

He was the sixth generation to live there. Twelve children had been born to his mother, all but two living to be eighty, and he was near that himself. We had to stoop to enter the dwelling. Inside, there were two rooms—one where the cow lived, accompanied by a duck and her family of ducklings and some chickens. In the other room, three cats sat by a peat fire, the smoke finding its way up and out through an opening in the thatch roof. The sun streamed through a small window in a long beam, blue with the peat reek. There was a bench or two, a bed, and some indications of housekeeping, but the piece of importance was the large teapot resting in the warm ash on the edge of the fire.

Donal asked us to sit down while he got tea, adding more leaves to the pot and water from the kettle. Then he found three mugs and poured out the blackest, strongest tea I had ever seen, or tasted. He needed to see the leaves in our cups if we would have him tell us what was ahead, so drink it all we must.

"Turn your cups slowly now, to the north, to the south, to the east, to the west," he said, "all the while making a wish."

It was a ritual that sent me back to the days at Hillhurst when Andy read the teacups.

Donal held my cup to his eye as if it were a spyglass, then he held Bill's. "There's not much difference for the two of you," he said, "and your fortune lies in the west, there's no doubt about that." He kept studying the cups with their leaves entangled at the bottom of each one. "It's good things that I see—a wee worry now and then, a removal. Here's a bargain to be closed, and some money to be made, and the worries will be over."

"When will all this happen?" I asked.

A smile twisted his face mysteriously. "Whoever talks of time when there's fortune ahead?"

Bill wanted to take Donal's picture before we left, and he agreed. "But wait till I get a wee duck in my hands." So Donal went back to his shieling and returned with a small duck cupped tenderly in his hands.

Over the path to the road we went, through heather and bracken. The long light of the afternoon deepened around us. The distant Coolins looked friendly. Portree shone like a jewel in a lapis and emerald setting.

The next morning we left for the west in a bus that rattled over as lonely a stretch of moor as we had yet seen. The few crofts and shielings were set wide apart as if nothing would induce their owners to leave their holdings for the compactness of a village. They looked self-sufficient. A line of Johnson's explained it: "The high hills which by hindering the eye from ranging forced the mind to find entertainment for itself."

Dunvegan, our immediate destination, was a small gray village stretched along a loch where the Atlantic came in rolling and crashing, only a few shades darker than the brooding clouds. We found a comfortable lodging with a peat fire to sit by while tea was in the making. What a tea—herrings, several kinds of bread, the best being scones and "girdle cakes," which we did justice to! We went to bed by candlelight. Rain pattered on the slate roof and wind shook the windows as if it wanted to come in. We read and studied the map, preparing ourselves for exploration.

Weather, no matter what it did, did not keep us from adventuring, but it did keep Bill from taking pictures, and we were glad to be able to sit by a fire at night and give our clothes a chance to dry out for the next day. We would set out early, whether the day was tristful or not, fortified by a breakfast of porridge with great clots of cream. Often, on a moor path, rabbits darted before us, and once a wren seemed to go ahead as if leading us. Seeing smoke rising from a vale, we were sure there was a village, but the smoke was spray "from waterfalls shooting upwards," just as the book had expressed it. A Royal Mail van might pass us on the road, or a farmer on horseback, and often a shepherd with his flock. We asked each one for a place known as "the big house." A man breaking stones gave us a lead that sent us down to the shore of Loch Varkasaig where we met a toothless crone milking her three black cows. She knew what we were talking about.

"When the mist clears off, you'll see it on yon far

shore, but it's no a house, it's an inn. If the folks there take a liking to you, they may put you up."

That afternoon the wind shifted and the sun came out with its magical effect. The loch glistened. The countryside came alive with color. Distantly we saw the outline of a big house standing high above the loch. We had a few miles to go to get back to our lodging, but a glowing sunset went with us and there was tea and a warm fire to cheer us. Bill made arrangements by phone and that night, before we went to bed, we looked out on a sky full of stars. The next day would see us at the "big house" where Fiona and her father had once lived.

"It's faired up for certain," we were assured as we left in the morning. The wind was strong from the north. The sun rode high in a cloudless sky. The moor danced with color. There was no question in my mind then but that Skye was the most beautiful place in the world.

When we reached Orbost, we knew that it was the end of our search, everything about the house and the surroundings tied with descriptions in the book. They evidently did take a liking to us, for there was a room "but for two nights only." That was all the time remaining to us, in any case.

"It's a pet day," the man at the desk said, "and tomorrow may be likewise. Make the most of it before the wind backs again."

Bill wanted the far shots first, because of the clarity of the light, so we climbed Heleval, mounting slowly through bracken and heather, crossing many burns and one with a fairy bridge. It was slow going, and the last bit was so steep with rock and scree that we could make it only on all fours, but once at the top

65

—what a view! All of Skye seemed spread below us, its great wings flung far out to sea. There were the Outer Hebrides, Lewis and Harris, perhaps even tiny St. Kilda lying against the horizon. Near were moors and villages and rocky coast with the blue Atlantic sparkling in the sunshine. Bill took pictures and pictures, and finally, when we retraced our downward way, I thought the camera must be shouting with the load of beauty it carried. Sunset drowned the distant Coolins in a plum-colored glow.

The next day Bill concentrated on scenes along the loch. The wind had shifted and clouds were massing, so he had what he longed to get into pictures. We rented a boat and went in search of the cave that figured so in the book. There were several caves on the Atlantic side of a small island, and Bill insisted on rowing in one so he could get a picture looking out of the cave entrance.

"Bill, remember what it said in the book. There may be no exit except to come out on the other side of time," I reminded him.

"And wouldn't that be a wee bit of an adventure," he replied.

So I rowed while he positioned his camera. It was dark inside the cave, the walls were dripping, the water, green and clear, felt like ice. I was relieved when we got back into the sunshine, rowing toward a small strip of white sand. Nothing would do for either of us but that we beach the boat and have a quick swim. The water was too cold to be endured for long, but it was invigorating.

"I think I've got all I need," Bill said as we looked at the stars that night and drank in the northern air.

When we packed our few belongings—Bill's films,

my notes, and the old worn copy of *The Treasure*— I felt like Fiona when she is told that she has found the treasure: ". . . the spirit of the island which you love. . . . You can walk now through the crowded city and never know it, for the wind from the heather will be about you where you go; you can stand in the tumult of men and never hear them, for round you will be the silence of your own sea. That is the treasure of the Isle of Mist; the island has given you of its soul."

September, 1937

It was not until we were back in London and the films were developed that we were sure—but, oh, were we sure! Bill went through the pictures very carefully and submitted to Oxford only the best, the absolute best. And Oxford was delighted. When the great W. W. Tarn (whom we never met) was shown them, his comment was a classic of understatement; but the check Bill received was not.

November, 1937

I am at my desk. With the stack of handwritten pages before me, I am as happy as Bill is with his camera. This is the time I like best—when the story is all there and I can go through it slowly, carefully, sure of the words I have used or, if uncertain, sure there can be a better one. And then there's the final phase of typing. With it, I'll endeavor to get as shapely a typescript as ever was placed on a publisher's desk. The title came as part of the whole, High Holiday. *How could it be anything else? Having satisfied myself that it is the best I can do, I read it to Bill.*

"I knew you would do it," he said.

XII, 6, 37

My darling —

This is a sort of special day, isn't it? At any rate I feel terribly excited. I am excited about —

1. you
2 - picture book
3 - High holiday & Wm Penn
4 - your desk
5 - chopping wood on _our_ farm
6 - Cornwall
7 - you.

Isn't it wonderful to be excited about such delectable things?

L.

1938

SHADOW OF WAR

January, 1938

It was just ten years ago I wrote in my journal that I was serving an apprenticeship, like a craftsman of old, working to gain necessary skills. Now, with High Holiday *finished, I feel that I have fulfilled my apprenticeship.*

March 11, 1938

What a day! I walk out of the office of A. and C. Black with a check and a contract in my pocket, and Hitler walks into Austria. The papers have huge headlines, and the world begins to wonder what the consequences will be. So the ordinary events of our lives go on, but against a darkening curtain.

Familiar with the type of books for young people that the Black firm published, I had sent *High Holiday* to them a few weeks before, never expecting to have a telephone call asking me to come in and talk with Mr. Archie Black. It was a pleasant conversation. He liked the book. Would I accept an outright offer of twenty-five pounds and publication within the year? Would I! It was my opening door. Even before I signed the contract, he said, "With your next book you will be on a royalty basis." Then he asked me if I would like to suggest an artist to do the jacket. "It must be something with the feeling of Switzerland and children, as there will be no illustrations in the book." I could think of no one better than Nora Unwin, a friend I had met recently, a graduate of the Royal College of Art. Mr. Black said he would get in touch with her.

When I told Bill about the arrangement I had come to with Mr. Black, he approved. "You may not like figures, but you have a sound sense of business." Somewhere, in the faraway past, my father had said similar words to me.

Bill is busy with another commission from Oxford, and I have my work on George MacDonald almost complete—the selection of his poems and a story of his life. My frequent teatime visits with his daughter, Lady Troup, have helped me, and through her I have drawn close to her father's vigorous mind, his wit, and his tenderness. The publisher to whom I would like to offer the book is W. Heffer and Sons in Cambridge. I write and ask for an appointment to see someone in the firm. A prompt reply gives me a date in less than a week!

March, 1938

We take off for a day in Cambridge. Bill has his camera for company and I have the box with my typescript. I even have a title, Gathered Grace. *The words are from a passage in* Donal Grant: *"The chosen agonize after the light; stretch out their hands to God; stir up themselves to lay hold upon God! These are they who gather grace, as the mountain-tops the snow, to send down rivers of waters to their fellows."*

Spring was in the world. The air was sweet, and the lovely lawns—the "Backs" through which the river Cam flows—were gay with daffodils. We agreed to meet for luncheon at the Bull in Trumpington Street, and I walked on to my appointment, past buildings mellowed by time while I was mellowed by sunshine. Presenting myself at the office, I told Mr. Heffer what I had done and placed the box on his desk, then I added that I hoped he would want to illustrate it with wood engravings by Nora Unwin. He looked at my pages casually, murmured something about "always having had a feeling for that old Scot," and asked if I would come back in the afternoon at three o'clock.

Bill and I had luncheon; then, with time to spare, we hired a boat and went rowing on the Cam between those incredibly green lawns and banks of flowers. Bill's camera was busy, and so was my mind, as I thought about *Gathered Grace* and its possible future.

When I went back to Mr. Heffer's office, he smiled and said, "We have decided to publish this. I will draw up a contract for you and write to Miss Unwin about the illustrations."

April, 1938

Being in the country always set us talking about when we would live in the country. Now, more and more, we thought about the dream we had been nurturing ever since we had tramped in the highlands of the Hudson. But where was that little farm to be? Bill decided to explore the possibilities in southern England while I went to Zurich to visit Father and Mother, who are staying there. Other dreams were coming true, why should not this one. Much as we loved London, we are not really city people, our tastes are too simple, our lives too quiet. Why not do now what we had been talking about—find a little farm, perhaps run a small guesthouse along with it, to draw our friends.

Meantime, it was Switzerland for me. Early in the morning, peering from the window of the train, I saw fields carpeted with flowers, dotted with mouse-colored cows, chalets with great stacks of wood, tidy villages. I could almost smell the air, rich with the manure that was being spread on some of the fields. I got to the Baur au Lac in time to join Mother and Father for breakfast on their balcony: croissants, black cherry jam, and what coffee! This was the day they "Burn the Bogg," and all Zurich was gay with festival.

By noon the streets had filled with people. Children in native dress, processions of Guilds in costume, each with its band, floats of flowers, and all preceded the Bogg, like a huge snowman complete with top hat, pipe, and besom, who was carried to his funeral pyre. They marched up and down the Bahnhofstrasse, then to the square near the lake. The Bogg was placed at the top of the pyre, the wood was set alight, flames licked high, the bells in the Gross Munster tolled, the bands played, and, when the flames touched the Bogg, rockets hidden within him went off. Soon he was all on fire and the crowd shouted "Bravo!" His besom, his pipe, his hat fell forward, and the Bogg himself soon went down to ash. And that was the end of winter!

Bill's letters from the farm where he was staying told of walks taken in buttercup fields, of tea in the garden with four dogs gamboling about him, of air filled with the smell of hawthorne and barnyard, of songs of birds and droning of bees swarming in the eaves of the old house. "Peace fills me as I sit here in the garden quietly purring, and a psalm of gratitude sings in me every morning when the sun comes into my room and announces another day. . . . I have long, practical talks with these people. They feel that if we started small, say twenty-five chickens and a cow or two—with a man to help with the milking, and a good size vegetable garden from which we could sell the surplus—we could make a go of it. With five pounds a week in cash coming in, we would be rich indeed. Then, as we got going, we could specialize in some particular field—sheep, perhaps, or honey. Tomorrow I am going out with a farm agent to see what is available. Yesterday I was helping John build his new bull pen, and he told me of his hopes and plans. I realized what every nail he drove meant to him. I am excited about *our* farm, and the enthusiasm I feel is not impetuous, but patient and deep-rooted."

I talked with Father and he shook his head.

"Don't you realize what is happening in the world? Don't you see the war clouds that are gathering?"

"Perhaps it won't happen."

"Your mother and I wish you would begin to think seriously about returning to America."

May, 1938

Before leaving Zurich, I had time for one climb, not a big mountain, but one big enough to give me the experience of walking backward in the year. Spring with its early flowers I left by the lake. In a few hundred feet the path was edged with snow and there were pussy willows, then tiny white crocuses looking like thimbles in the sod. The lake below me was startlingly blue, the distant mountains white walls reflecting the sun. The only sounds were the dull splits and crashes of avalanches far away. On my way down, the sight of an occasional blue gentian caught my eye, peering out from the rocks as if to test the coming warmth. Back at the lake, I was in spring again. I wondered when I reread my notes, if someday I would feel that I was walking backward in my life.

I told Bill about my talk with Father, and he agreed that we must think seriously, but so much was happening now.

July, 1938

Our holiday was determined by a letter from Bertha Miller of *The Horn Book*. She had long thought that there should be a new edition of the Tregarthen legends of North Cornwall, books published at the turn of the century and made well known by the fact that Queen Mary read them aloud to her children. Could we manage a few days in Cornwall to see what we could find?

"Sleuthing again," Bill said, "but think of the pictures!"

The flat and Bara were left in Phyllis' care, and Nora agreed to come in every afternoon, when Phyllis would have tea for her. It was a day-long train journey through summer-sweet English country to the town of Padstow on the Camel River. There was just enough light when we arrived for Bill to see the picture possibilities—a small quaint town on the edge of Bodmin Moor, a wide sweep of river and glistening sands with the tide out, great towering cliffs where the river emptied into the Atlantic. Beyond our range of sight, but within walking reach, was Tintagel and the country rich in Arthurian lore.

We began our search the next morning, but no one at the inn or the post office remembered anyone of the name we were seeking. Then someone recalled that Enys Tregarthen was Nellie Sloggett, "the little cripple." We found her stone in the churchyard: "*Nell Age 72 Died 1923*," and we found our way down Dinas Lane to the house where she had lived and been cared for by her cousin, Maude Rawle. That first tea with Miss Rawle was not the last, but it was memorable, with saffron buns, rolls split and covered with clotted cream, and pasties. She would not tell us what was in them, for she said it was well known that the Devil would not come into Cornwall for fear of being put into a pie. During the days that followed she answered our many questions, told us about her cousin, produced the books we were seeking and, as well, a small trunk filled with unpublished manuscripts, which she insisted upon giving to us. Many hours I spent alone with Miss Rawle while Bill roamed with his camera.

On our last afternoon, over cups of tea, she told us a story of her father, who had run away to sea at the age of nine. For sixty years he had followed the sea, returning often to Padstow with treasures from far countries and for brief visits with his family. "Once," she told us, "when he was captain of his ship, he was told of a ghost who was frightening his men. He knew that if it kept up, there would soon be trouble, so he called the sailors on deck one morning, took out his heavy iron pistol and said to them, 'You know I'm a good shot. If it's a man, I can't miss him, if it's a ghost, I can't hit him.' From that day on, the ghost was never heard of again."

Cornwall, the search for Enys Tregarthen, the friendship with Miss Rawle, had given us treasure beyond telling. When we left her, the box of manuscripts carried carefully by Bill, we tried to thank her.

"You're welcome," she said, "I don't need them."

But something more was to crown our Cornish stay. When we got back to the inn, there was a package that had come in the afternoon post. It was from A. and C. Black, my copy of *High Holiday*. I showed Bill the dedication: *"To William—Because we have climbed mountains together."*

Nothing would do but that I start reading it aloud to Bill that night, while a rain-laden wind swept in from the sea and a fire of coals whispered warmth.

"It's like being at Heimeli again," Bill said.

August, 1938

Phyllis might smile when we returned and Bara might wag his tail gleefully, but London was different —rumors of war, headlines in the papers, trenches being dug in Hyde Park for shelters, gas masks being issued, and leaves starting to fall because the summer had been dry and hot.

September, 1938

Gathered Grace commenced its journey into the world. It was a handsome book, rich because of Mac-Donald, beautiful with Nora's engravings. I took a copy to Lady Troup. We said nothing about the world, for at this moment the book was her world and mine; but the strain of the past weeks had been hard on everyone, and there were tears in her eyes when she kissed me good-by.

Bland, warm, and beautiful was the late September day as I walked back to Edwardes Square; it seemed to belie all else that was going on in the world. Leaves were still falling, and the smoke from many burning piles hung in the air, scenting it. I could not escape the headlines as I walked along Kensington High Street. They screamed and newsmen called: what will the Prime Minister come back with this time? He had gone again to Munich to meet with Hitler, hoping to achieve peace. I felt as if I were walking in a dream, so terrible it all was. The end of the world might be at hand or, if the torch of the spirit was raised a little higher, a little longer, it might mark the beginning of a new world. The tension that had been mounting for the past year was so great. How much longer could it go on without something snapping?

When Bill and I got home from the theater there were crowds poring over newspapers, buses racing. It seemed like a mad world. The midnight news said that unless a miracle happened before morning the tide of events would flow only one way. By 4 A.M. the miracle had happened. Neville Chamberlain had returned, with his umbrella and one more concession.

September 30, 1938

Peace is assured, not only here but everywhere, not only for this day but for all time. That is what I say and Bill shakes his head. Two men have met each other in conference. Today is the hinge on which the progress of the world can turn. The gas masks, the trenches in Hyde Park, the sandbags, the big antiaircraft guns erected so hastily have all become scenery in a play, soon to be shifted. We can look on them with eyes of interest instead of horror. Armageddon came near, but it did not engulf us.

The sun is streaming through the windows. I find I can smile again. Phyllis sings at her work and brings flowers "because you have been so kind to me this week." In my heart—a deepening desire to dedicate myself to peace. I can and will do all possible through my work—instantly and forever—to make sure that where I am there is peace.

That night, after Phyllis had left and we were sitting by the fire with our coffee, Bill started to talk about "our farm."

"Where, Bill? In Kent?"

"No, in New England."

I must have looked my surprise.

"If there is war," Bill went on quietly, "and we stay here with England through her agony, we will never go home. Having endured, we would feel we should stay to help rebuild."

"But peace has just been assured. Why do you say 'if'?"

He shook his head. "It is not peace, it is time that has been given. We won't go soon, for we both have commitments to fill, but by next summer we should be making other plans. Our lease will be up then, you will have finished the book Mr. Black wants, and I will have had time to complete my work for Oxford."

October, 1938

Perhaps it was the release from the tension of the days, but Bill had a dark time—the room with curtains drawn, the quiet as nearly as it could be achieved, the pain that nothing could lessen. We had time to talk, much time, after the intensity of the first few days, and I was more and more willing to think of a sometime future in our own country. I was even beginning to feel a little pull of the heart. Perhaps I was seeing with Bill's eyes.

So long as we lived in England, we would be living half a life, for we are Americans. England mellowed us, tempered us, disciplined us. It was like a sheltering garden where the small plants of our lives put down their roots; now we were about ready to be transplanted. The winds might blow stronger in America, the light might be sharper, the heat and cold more intense, but we would return with what England had shown us we could do and were doing, with our joint and separate talents. We would find a place in the country, have that little farm, and carry on with our work. We started to make a list of what we wanted to find.

"You must go to America and make a quick survey," Bill said when the dark time passed and he was himself again.

With that ahead, we made our plans.

November, 1938

I was setting out like Columbus to discover America, but unlike Columbus, I knew it was there. I wanted to discover the answer to a big question looming before us. Could we find the way, not the place yet, but the feeling of a life that we could fit into with what we had and had not? As the S.S. *Normandie* glided on over smooth seas through a moon-full night, I wondered.

Five days later I came on deck at 9 A.M. and cried

inwardly with joy—sunshine and a glittering sea dotted with little boats, and the big ship approaching harbor in a slow majestic way! The city was cloaked in a pearly haze; tugs and ferries were going about their business; and there was Liberty, holding her torch high. It was a thrill to see her, and I felt a surge of loyalty rise up in me. This is my land! The lofty buildings told me to look up as if to be ready to face and accept a challenge. We docked at noon and I was soon through the customs, into a bevy of friends and a world as new and different as any Columbus came upon.

Loyola said, "You've grown up."

Eunice said everything in her embrace.

Three days in New York and how could I ever sort out the swift impressions to take back to Bill! There were so many, they came so quickly and they were so conflicting. Shabbiness in many of the side streets, grandeur along Fifth Avenue, and how could people possibly need or want the things the shops were filled with! Unbelievable comfort in a hotel room, food superb, from pancakes at Child's to the best at Longchamps. People were well-dressed and moved with a sort of precision. But the noise, the restlessness, and the haste! Everything was bigger and better, but was there happiness? I looked at the faces of the people I passed in the street and often there was a harried expression, almost a hunted one. What were they pursuing or being pursued by, and why were they all in such a hurry? Everyone talked, but did anyone listen? There was such bitterness against Roosevelt for what he had done, and such bitterness against England for what she had not done.

People quoted authorities: "Dorothy Thompson says . . ." "Walter Lippmann says . . ." And I cried inwardly, "But what do you say?" The depression had left its mark, evident in despair. I heard of people who had "lost everything" and one day I was introduced to a woman who "has nothing," but her clothes, her manner, and the car she drove said otherwise. Much of the conversation I was involved in or overheard had to do with politics, graft, drink, corruption, disease, and underlying it was rebellion against the present administration. "What we need is a leader" came like a theme song. Germany was saying that and got a Hitler. Perhaps it was not a leader so much as a unifying element that was needed. Independence made this country, but in a bus I was shocked when the driver said, "Move away from the door, please," and the passenger replied, "I will not; I'll stay where I am."

The Ellises, old friends with whom we had kept in touch, took a day off to show me the nearby country. I was amazed at the speed with which we left the city —the motor parkways so safe, swift, unobstructed where the stream of cars moved like a metallic river. There were frequent signs saying that the speed limit was 40 mph, and I murmured once to Charles, "Aren't you going seventy?"

"Oh, nobody pays any attention to those signs," he answered cheerfully.

From the backseat Louise spoke softly, "We've forgotten how to be a law-abiding people."

Once we were off the parkway and onto a lesser road, the difference stunned me—signs, advertising, gas stations, diners, dance places, stores, all adding up to shabby confusion. But we left that road for one that passed through a succession of charming villages where a green was graced by tall trees and bordered by gracious houses. Charles drew up to an unprepossessing little inn, where we stopped for luncheon. The food was delicious, everything was simple, clean, attractive, and served with an engaging friendliness.

After luncheon we strolled around the village green. Charles pointed to a small sign, REAL ESTATE, and suggested that we see what might be available. "Just in case you decide to settle here."

We went in. It was a delightful office and the owner was all smiles at the sight of a prospect. I saw a sign that irked me—Gentile neighborhood.

"What does that mean?" I asked.

He looked me over closely, then said with the kind of smile that comes only from the lips, "Just what it says. Coming from New York, as I see you are, you will appreciate that kind of neighborhood."

It was hard for me to turn slowly enough to leave that office.

Charles and Louise followed me out. "What's the matter, don't you feel well?"

"I'm not looking at any houses here," and I tried to explain. "Don't you know what Hitler is doing in Germany? We're not much better here if we have notices like that."

The villages were lovely with their greens, their stately houses and steepled churches, their public libraries and schools. The air was fresh and the people moved with quieter pace and more serene expressions. This was the America I was seeking, the America to which I belonged and yet there was prejudice here, where all races and peoples are supposed to merge as they will in the Kingdom of Heaven. I was haunted by a question: has this land a soul, or has it sold its soul to the automobile, to self-gratification, to "progress"?

Always there is another side. I was aware of

warmth, spontaneity, and a politeness that charmed me: a perfect stranger would hold a door open for me; in an elevator men with hats on whipped them off when a woman entered, and squeezed themselves together to let her out first. Introduced to new people I felt that I was instantly embraced, taken into their lives; in England it took so long to develop a friendship, but once it happened it was forever.

The efficiency bewildered me. One day in New York and I accomplished what would have taken three in London; even to the way books arrived at the New York Public Library desk almost before my request had gone through. At the British Museum I could settle down and read the *Daily Telegraph* before the books I asked for came to my cubicle. And I was fascinated by the way people championed causes almost before they found out whether they were worth championing.

Before I left for Boston I had dinner with Loyola Sanford. She was unhurried, ready to listen. She knew about *High Holiday*. She knew that once started I would continue. "But life moves so fast here," I said. "Can I ever fit into a world of writing?"

"A book must be good to sell, first to a publisher, then to the public, because a book is a business proposition."

I told her that I was uneasy at the thought of writing for a market that demanded so much realism.

"With many people success must be instant or not at all." She smiled in the way that ten years ago had given me confidence. "You are willing to wait and keep on working. You'll survive, and on your own terms."

Boston was different from New York—the people, the pace—and I began to have a distinct feeling of belonging. I had already had several meetings with editors, generally over luncheon or tea. The sense of hurry had abated. My first appointment was with Bertha Miller, editor of *The Horn Book*. She was delighted at the report I brought her of the Tregarthen legends. When I described Bill's pictures and how they set the scenes, she clapped her hands together. She was gentle and charming, a small person with a quavery voice, but what wisdom! She had the joy of a child in little things, and she made me feel that I could accomplish what I set heart and hand to. She told me of some people to see in New York and said she would write letters to them ahead of my next visit.

"Helen Ferris at Stokes, May Massee at Viking, they are great names, but don't feel intimidated. Your work can stand." She gave me many helpful leads and said there would be much I could do for *The Horn Book* "when you and your husband come back to stay."

Maude Meagher, editor of *World Youth*, was interested in some of my ideas, as was Barbara Nolen of *Story Parade*. Very meaningful was the time spent with Margaret Williamson, Ethel C. Ince, and Roscoe Drummond of the *Christian Science Monitor*. The paper had been carrying a good deal of my work, and they could use more—essays with Bill's pictures for the Home Forum page, the Kilts stories, book reviews, and interviews for the magazine section. I had several long talks with Miss Williamson and I savored every word. She was a large, calm person with an almost impassive face. She gave me the feeling of having quiet command of her thoughts and her life. She put me in mind of Miss Russell, my long-ago mentor, for she was teaching me so much. I told her that when a piece of mine was published on her page, I compared it with the copy I had sent her.

"And you found some changes?"

"Yes, a word here, a mark of punctuation there, even a reconstruction of a sentence. Always you have improved me."

"Then you have not minded, have not felt I took liberties?"

"On the contrary. You're an editor, you know."

"Some people don't trust an editor."

What was I to say except that I'm not that kind of person?

The Atlantic Ocean seemed to be shrinking. Soon I could see that it might not exist at all, as the work opening up for me could be better done here.

Ann, friend from the year at Oaksmere, suggested a day in the country. We left Boston easily and drove through such storied places as Lexington and Concord, then Groton, and into southern New Hampshire. The country was beautiful in its late-fall dress. The fields were brown as a deer's coat, the woods gray, the line of hills before us deeply blue. The villages we went through were neat and self-respecting. It was warm enough for a picnic, so we left the car and walked through a woods in brilliant sunshine, leaves crackling underfoot, wind surging in the treetops. We found a brook racing over stones, and it seemed part of the vigor of the day. Somehow there was a newness, a freshness, a sense of possibility over everything. I felt myself becoming a part of it. To the west, one mountain was like a pyramid against the sky. No other mountain is like that. I did not ask Ann what its name was, I knew. Bill and I had climbed Monadnock and looked from its height on a countryside that pleasured us.

Thanksgiving, 1938

Snow had been falling softly all day and the countryside was beautiful in its mantle of white. The air was sharp and deliciously cold, and I was aware of the tremendous vitality all around me. The house at Hillhurst Farm had always been expandable and now it had need to be more so than ever. The assemblage of family at dinner was tremendous. The marrieds had children, and they were all there. Father carved a big roast turkey at his end of the table and Mother a boiled turkey with oyster dressing at her end. So easily I seemed to slip back into my old groove. I listened to the talk, and it was of politics for that was a major concern, the movies, the radio, sports, rackets, and wages—up to five dollars an hour, and where will it end—"Working people are never satisfied." The older generation saw a sort of demoralizing madness in all that was happening; my generation, with Bob as spokesman, saw an inevitability and felt that good would eventually shape from it. They asked me what I thought. Whatever I said, it was tinged with England, and no one is happy about England. After dinner, the younger ones went out to play in the snow and that gave more opportunity for talk in the living room by a blazing fire.

Bob, always my comfort, spoke of the books, Bill's and mine, and said, "Building a literary reputation must be easier in England than here."

"Why?"

"You've got to be sensational here, and you'll never be that."

Father said, "In many ways you're better off in England, but I'd like to see you back here."

December, 1938

I had much to do with my remaining two days in New York, but I took my time walking slowly up Fifth Avenue and strolling into the shops with their multitude of lovely things. So much was bright and gay, as if to catch the eye and the moment rather than meet a need. I did go into Sulka's and found a most handsome foulard tie for Bill.

Appointments following on Mrs. Miller's letters filled my day. A publisher for the Cornish legends was first on my list, then to find someone interested in *Gathered Grace*. At the New York Public Library, Anne Carroll Moore was positively excited about the legends and felt that once they were in print they would become an important part of folklore. She made me feel that I was bearing precious jewels, but when I talked with her about *Gathered Grace*, her attitude was different; she had always had a frank dislike for MacDonald. So I called on Helen Ferris at Stokes to tell her about the Tregarthen tales. Her interest was real, real enough for her to say that she would make an offer as soon as they came to her desk; then I told her about the photographs that set the scenes, and she lost interest. No photographs, they distract. I said no more. To me the whole is greater than its parts and the pictures that linked the Cornish land with the words were an important part of the book.

I made a courtesy call at Oxford University Press, because Grace Hogarth, with Oxford in London, wanted me to establish a relationship with the New York office, and I talked with Harper's about an American edition of the MacDonald. Perhaps they were just being polite, but they appeared interested. Holiday House was next, but it didn't take me long to realize that not one of the three editors I talked with would feel that anything I might do "would be for them." My last call was at Viking with May Massee. What a noble person she was and what authority she had! But I doubted that I could ever please her. In a curious way I was retracing my steps of ten years ago, and, just as I felt then, I felt as surely now that I would carry my own banner high, no matter who said what.

New York was filled with contradictions—so beautiful, so cruel; so rich, so poor; so filled with possibility, so crushing. A taxi driver that morning couldn't be kind enough. He told me he was always on the lookout for people who needed help. "Like you, when you flagged me down. I've got a bundle of joy at home and I want her to be proud of her daddy when she grows up." Then he went on with more of his life story, and I wished that I could have gone farther with him. I could imagine myself writing about him. I didn't have a chance to tell him, he talked so fast and so much, that the reason I hailed him was because I had asked directions from three people: the first person didn't speak English and merely shrugged his shoulders, the second sent me in the wrong direction, and the third growled such a gruff answer that I trembled for moments afterward. But he made up for all of them.

That last night I had dinner with Mildred and Peter, both so sane and sensible, and their home was all a home should be—a haven of peace and beauty. It was late when they took me to the ship, and as we taxied through the quiet streets there was a white moon in a blue-velvet sky playing hide-and-seek with us between the tall buildings. We said good-by at the dock. Once aboard I stood by the rail a long time until I felt the ship begin to move. When I went down to my cabin it was filled with fragrance from a bowl of flowers, violets and lily of the valley and mignonette.

"They came by cable, madame," the steward said.

So much has been confusing these past weeks, but if there is one thing of which I am sure, it is love.

1939

CLIMBING HIGHER

January, 1939

London seems very gray and damp. Even with the modicum of central heating that we have at Edwardes Square I have not felt warm, really warm, since I returned. On threatening days, the weather forecast often says that "a depression is bearing down from Iceland." But it is not entirely from that quarter. The trenches are covered over in the parks; the gas masks have been put away in drawers. People are more reserved than ever. A smile seemed so simple in America, whether you knew a person or not; but not so here, not now. Few use the word, but all know what is impending: war. The tension of last September has returned, and it is sharper. A retort comes more easily than a compliment in conversation. How long can people live under this somber, brooding cloud? How long can people endure uncertainty?

And yet, with us in any case, there was reason for satisfaction. We looked at the tiny portion of the book-case that held our own books: Bill's two picture books from Warne, *The Frog, the Penny, and the Big Black Tree* and *Dennis the Donkey,* and at the two photographic books he has done for Oxford, *First Friends* and *First Animal Friends,* and the beautiful *Treasure of the Isle of Mist;* beside them stand *High Holiday* and *Gathered Grace.*

The reviews that had been coming to Oxford on the picture books were rewarding, and from sources like *Time and Tide*, the *New Statesman*, the *Observer*, the *Manchester Guardian*. All along I had known that Bill, in his pictures, had an eye for the story, and with that he had caught the wonder of children in the things of their world. About these first books for babies, reviewers said they "tell their own stories in photographs that are direct, simple, uncluttered with distracting detail . . . an original departure from the conventional . . . done by a skillful photographer with artistry and humor but with none of the tricks of modern photography . . . clean, polished, unpretentious with a simplicity that is a mark of high technical dexterity."

Those were words to savor!

We knew where the next adventure would take us: Iceland! Nora had just returned from a visit there with her cousin who was married to an Icelander. She was ecstatic about the country—the people, the history, and the possibilities for pictures. Her sketchbooks were full, and when she told Bill about the cloud formations that build up and sweep down low in an embrace of the land, he was ready to get film and leave the next day. I saw Iceland as the setting for the further adventures of Michael and Meredith Lamb. The title had already proclaimed itself—*Climbing Higher*.

April, 1939

Days of wind and sleet were followed by mild days and we realized that the marvel of an English spring was again at hand, and it would be our last, of that we had no doubt. In fact, our thoughts went so often now to the little farm in New Hampshire that we started leaving notes around the flat to each other, "Bulletins from Windrush Farm." "The doe has just brought her fawns to the edge of the pasture." "There's a blueberry pie cooling on the kitchen windowsill." "Bara and Wee Maggie have taken their puppies for a stroll." Phyllis, dusting, found one of Bill's notes and asked me whatever it meant, "The hens are now laying 3 1/3 eggs apiece per day."

"However can that be?"

"Anything can happen in a story," I explained, "and these are a story we are telling each other."

In the Square, aconites had replaced snowdrops, and crocuses were opening. Such lovely sights came as an assurance that no matter what is happening with people, nature follows her ordered way.

We were just back from one of our walking weekends, this time in the Cotswolds. Never before had the country seemed so beautiful, poignantly beautiful. The villages, each one a pleasant walking distance from the other, looked tidier than ever. The Windrush River, no more really than an oversize brook, was pursuing its course. The footpaths were Bara's joy, and ours. The dogs we met frequently along the way had interesting confrontations with each other, then responded to their owners' voice or call, as Bara did to Bill's warble. The inn at Broadway was all that an inn should be, as we had learned from previous visits.

The path we decided to follow Saturday morning led through Checkers, the prime minister's residence, and along it spring was everywhere, in primroses and birds, fragrance and melody. How it happened I do not know, but somewhere along the way I had put down Bill's beloved binoculars and failed to pick them up again, for I realized at some point that we did not have them. And they are essential to Bill, even for very near things. I was contrite, he was philosophical.

That night at the Golden Cockerel, another walker came up to us with the binoculars in his hand. "Could these be yours?" he asked.

With so many things we did now, we said, "This is the last time," and yet the ache of parting was eased, for a "first time" was ahead: the seeking and finding of a permanent home, the settling in, the putting down of roots that have been pulled up many times. And with this journey Bara could cross the ocean with no quarantine ahead. He would be with us as part of the new life, and the "wee wifie" that has figured so in my series of Kilts stories would be a reality, once we found that little white farmhouse on a New Hampshire hillside.

May, 1939

We packed everything away that we could do without for the time being. Up to the moment the movers came to take things to storage, Phyllis was with us, smiling, sturdy, and so reliable. She handled with care the Crown Derby tea service that Bill and I had just bought, wanting to have in our new home something so very English, something that would accompany the silver tea set and remind us always of that hour in English life when tea reigns. We made another purchase, at Story's, a small Persian rug, brick and blue, my favorite colors, almost carrying out in shades, on the floor, what the Crown Derby will add to the tea table. Bill packed the china with careful hands as we looked ahead to the time when it would next be used. Where and when would that be?

93

The next day was so beautiful, soft and sunny, that we called a halt to our labors, told Phyllis to go to her sister's and forget about dinner. We were going to go to Richmond Park for one last walk in a loved place with a bag of bread crusts to feed the deer. Bara could always sense an adventure and was like a bouncing ball when Bill clipped his lead to his collar and we set out for High Street and the bus that would take us to Richmond. He walked properly beside Bill then, not really needing his lead at all, and was a model of decorum when we bought his ha'penny ticket so he could sit beside us on the bus. In the park there were a few people enjoying the day as we were, a few dogs greeting each other and romping together, then responding to their owners, and a few deer approaching cautiously and accepting daintily the bread offered to them.

I can't bear to write this down and yet somehow I must, for it was a part of our lives and of this tense year we all lived through. We had turned back and were going toward the bus stop because, though the days were lengthening, we felt there was good reason to be home early. There were still books to be packed and many things to be done. Behind us a man was walking with a large dog. I scarcely noticed him, and Bara was completely unaware when, with a medley of throaty sounds, the dog suddenly bore down upon Bara.

Bara wheeled quickly and wagged his tail, lifting his long nose in query; but friendship was not the big dog's intent. He seized Bara by the neck and shook him violently, then dropped him. Bara made some small sounds and, valiant Scot that he was, tried to struggle to his feet. The man came running up, attached a chain to his dog's collar, and said, "Sorry." Sometimes an

English voice can make that word sound more like "Soddy." "I hope your dog isn't hurt," then went off.

Bara was bleeding terribly, but his eyes were open, and when Bill reached down to pick him up, he did his best to wag his tail. Bill folded him in his coat and carried him. It was not a bus we took, but a taxi, and to the nearest veterinarian. Bara died in Bill's arms, so we did not go to the vet after all, but to Edwardes Square. That night, wrapping Bara in a canvas sheet, we buried him under some bushes in the Square where he had often buried bones. I thought of what Lotte had said about Sinna in Gstaad. Now there was something of us that would always be a part of England.

The war that was as yet no war had given us a casualty. It was all part of the tension that could break anywhere. "Sometimes animals sense things before humans," Bill said.

June, 1939

We sailed on the midnight tide out of Edinburgh, and the adventures we had I gave to Michael and Merry as the new book grew in me. Four weeks were almost like eight, for, at this time of the year, this far north, there was daylight around the clock. Nora had given us open sesame to her friends. On the ship we read more about Iceland, studied the map, and tried to become familiar with useful phrases from our Icelandic-English book. Bill chuckled when he read one of the phrases to me: "How am I ever going to find this when I need it —'I have fallen off my horse.'"

It was a bare, beautiful land and a friendly people. Daily adventures do not make a book, or the kind I wanted *Climbing Higher* to be, but the day when we were

95

on Hekla something happened and the book began to come together.

We were two days away from Reykjavik, on sturdy ponies, horses to the Icelanders, with a guide. We spent the previous night at a pastor's house and left in the morning to climb Hekla, a mountain not quite five thousand feet high and a volcano, too. It was a misty day and the pastor warned us that Hekla was "shy" and did not welcome visitors. Our guide, with far fewer words of English than we had of Icelandic, became more and more cautious as we drew near the summit. It was hard to tell at that point whether the mist we saw was just that or smoke from the volcano which is not entirely inactive.

The ponies had been left in a corral of stones and the last few hundred feet were to be done on foot. We must have been quite near the summit when our guide suddenly said we would go no farther. It was not safe in the thickening mist. I was so disappointed that I kept asking him if we couldn't take the chance. He shook his head, folded his arms across his chest, and nodded in the direction down the way we had come.

"He knows," Bill said, "and don't you remember from Switzerland, we put our safety in Fritz's hands and had to accept his way?"

Aching with chagrin at being worsted by a mountain, even though it was a volcano with a reputation for being temperamental, I turned with Bill and we followed the guide back to where we had left the ponies. But, and this is the important part, at the foot of Hekla we met an Icelander with whom we talked for a few minutes. He had a story to tell. Had we not turned back when we did, we would have missed him, and he (unwittingly) gave me what I needed: the solution to the problem I had set myself. The book now had a plot! In my little bed in the pastor's tiny house I wrote this down, because out of apparent defeat came victory. Looking out of my window and across the flat green field I could see Hekla, no longer swathed in mist, but clothed in a rosy light from the sun which had just dipped down in the west. Instead of being angry, I thought, "Oh, Hekla, you have given me so much more than the view from your summit!"

The night before we left, we did achieve a summit —and all by ourselves—Esja, the great flat-topped mountain across the bay from Reykjavik. We left about nine o'clock and climbed until midnight, had our thermos of coffee and little cakes, then gazed wide-eyed at the world below and around us. The sun had disappeared and there was a kind of half-light for an hour or so. We started down as dawn began to touch distant heights and far-reaching sea.

July, 1939

"What was Iceland like?" Marguerite asked when I called her on the phone from Edinburgh.

"Space filled with light," I said.

"Didn't you miss trees?"

"No."

Traveling down to London on the Flying Scotsman and looking from the train windows, I wanted to push the great trees out of the way, and yet they are such a part of England.

We settled in at Jordans, a guest house in Buckinghamshire. Oddly enough, some of it is made from the

97

timbers of the *Mayflower* which brought the Pilgrims to our land more than three centuries ago. I had just one month to do a whole book, so I worked busily. Much of it was already in my notebooks. I had a history of Iceland, the maps we used, my friend the dictionary, and what helped most of all, Bill's pictures as he got them developed.

The Quaker Meeting House where William Penn worshiped was across a little space of green from the garden of our hostelry. I liked to go there at times to sit and think, or perhaps just sit and be thought through. The story was writing itself and I was reliving our glorious adventure. The typing would be the hardest part, but my machine was in good order, with a new ribbon, and I had a ream of the best quality paper. In between stints of work we walked.

I think we discovered every footpath, visited every hamlet within ten miles of Jordans, but no joyful little dog capered beside us. I still ached about Bara, and if I thought too much, I grew angry.

Bill said, "Life has its hard times for us all, which we must be able to face."

I think he knew more about this than I, than many of us do.

Time did not quite run out on me, for I delivered *Climbing Higher* to Mr. Archie Black on the promised date, and I left his office with a proper contract in my hand.

August, 1939

A ship was throbbing under me again. The S.S. *Nieuw Amsterdam,* a crowded ship, not tourists this time, but people like ourselves who had lived abroad and were now returning. Our furniture might be in the hold, or it might follow on a cargo ship to be stored in Boston until we found our home.

After Jordans, we had stayed with the Unwins at Manor Wood in Surrey, and Nora drove us to Southampton to meet the *Nieuw Amsterdam*. Saying good-by to her was a big wrench, for we had worked together now on three books and would like to work together on many more. What was ahead no one knew, only that war clouds became more menacing with every day. Nora put a bunch of carnations in my hands and it was not dew that glistened on them. I'll never be able to smell that fragrance without thinking of the time when the tender left to take its freight of people out to the ship standing at sea. Nora stood among the great crowd on the dock, waving to us as we waved back to her. Do we never realize what a person means until a parting comes?

Mother and Father and Bob met us at the dock and the hours with them in New York were warm and real. I kept thinking of Stevenson's lines—

> Home is the sailor, home from the
> sea,
> And the hunter home from the hill.

Yes, we are home. Before the family left on the train for Buffalo, Father put in my hands a sealed envelope. "This is for you and Bill when you have found your house."

We took no time to see people in New York, to look up friends, do any business, for every moment now was to count. As soon as we got to Boston, we changed stations and took the train to Peterborough, New Hampshire. We were going home.

After breakfast at the Peterborough Tavern, Bill went to Steele's to get a paper. I waited, for as soon as he returned, the next half hour would be taken up in reading the news to him.

"You won't need to," he said, "I can read this much." He pointed to the two-inch high headline: WAR.

Why weren't people crying the news on street corners? Why weren't bells tolling? Why weren't—I thought of all the things that would have been happening, probably were happening right then, in London, when I realized—it was not "our war," not yet, anyway. I read more of the fine type, and the editorials, which Bill always wanted to hear. The news came as no surprise, perhaps it was a relief, though filled with anguish.

We walked across Main Street and called on a real estate man, Mr. Bishop. We told him what we were seeking, though we had begun to modify our thought of a working farm. At the way Bill's sight was going, we knew now that we could realize only a portion of the dream we had held for so long. Bill took the list we had made from his pocket and showed it to Mr. Bishop—an old farm with a small house and a barn, open fields, woodland, a brook, nearby hills and lakes, walking distance to a village, good road, four-season year. The list was studied carefully, then Mr. Bishop said it should not be too hard to find something that would suit us. He did not mention price, nor did we.

October, 1939

During the gentle days of autumn that became ever more golden, I felt in two worlds—a part of me was in England, the other part was in Peterborough. Mr. Bishop felt that to familiarize us with the countryside was more important, at the moment, than to find a house, so he drove us around almost every afternoon. He did manage to show us property as we looked at distant hills and nearby lakes. Some houses were beyond our means, others beyond our needs. A few were worth thinking about, even a second visit; but the perfect one did not appear. Bill assured me that we would know it when we saw it.

It seemed sensible to rent a furnished house for the winter, and Margaret Perry in Hancock had such a house. When approached, she was blunt and generous. "Have it for a month or a year. We won't bother with a lease, just a check now and then until you find your own place and don't need this anymore."

The house was small, old, charming, a mile or so out from the village. It would give us a chance to settle in to the countryside, to learn about the weather, to have quiet when it was needed. The eye attacks were becoming more frequent and more devastating.

December 31, 1939

I've just performed the ritual I do every year at this time since I started really earning. In my little ledger, the left column lists work sent out; in the right are the amounts paid when work is accepted. The columns now almost match each other, and the total, in dollars, not pounds, begins to look quite respectable.

1940–1942

SHIELING IN NEW HAMPSHIRE

March, 1940

We were still looking at houses and I was forever falling in love with impossible ones. I could not see the disadvantages in a darling house whose brook had a swimming pool and whose beams spoke of a time when fires smoked; but Bill could. It was too remote and the acreage was more than we would know what to do with. Reluctantly I saw the place through his eyes. There was another, a little white house that lay in the lap of a hill. We made several inspections, even spent a day there on our own, drank water from its well, peered in the windows. I was enamored, but Bill felt it was not the one. I got annoyed and asked "Why?"

"It is on a dirt road that may or may not be improved. Do you know the difficulties that might impose in winter or in March mud season?"

"But—"

"The village over the hill is a small one and that might prove stifling."

"But—"

"The land has been abandoned for a long time. It

would be costly to bring it back."

Bill had all the arguments, but to me the house was a dream of beauty. When he explained to Mr. Bishop "our" (I wanted him to say "his") thinking, Mr. Bishop agreed with him.

There was another house high on a hill, on a black road, in good condition but needing some alterations. I was ready to set up housekeeping with a blanket roll and a coffeepot.

"It's a long way from any village or town," Bill said quietly. "That may not mean anything now, but for year-round living and for all our years, it is best to be less remote."

I didn't want to give that house up, but I did, marveling always at how much farther Bill saw than I did. I was impatient. Bill was calm.

"We know what we want. We see it clearly with our inward eyes. Wait until we see it outwardly. We will."

"How can you ever be so sure?"

"Because I've seen this happen too many times to doubt."

Writing time was hard to come by, and I longed for the days when I could get back to my chosen work, but I had put the Cornish tales in order and with Bill's pictures they were ready to be presented to a publisher. *Climbing Higher* had come out in England and an American edition with the title *Quest in the Northland* had been taken by Knopf. There was every reason for me to go to New York "on business." Wilda Linderman, a friend we had come to know in Peterborough, gave me a letter to Richard Walsh, president of the John Day Company. He had published books by her father, Frank B. Linderman. I wrote to Mr. Walsh and received an invitation to call on him "when next in New York."

April, 1940

Bill's conviction that when a thing is right we know it, happened with Mr. Walsh. I had sent ahead the Cornish tales, now called *Piskey Folk*, with a collection of Bill's pictures. I had no sooner sat down in Mr. Walsh's office than he told me they wanted to do the book. "Those photographs," he exclaimed, "what they do to make the land real!" It was a delightful hour and thoroughly profitable for both Bill and me. Before I left, Mr. Walsh said he would like me to meet his wife, Pearl Buck.

I felt as if I were being introduced to royalty when he took me in to her office. She was beautiful and commanding, like a queen on a throne. I thought I would be tongue-tied in her presence, but I wasn't, because she asked me a question that I could answer.

"You write? Tell me, do you develop your characters so that what happens could only happen to them in the lives they are living, or do you have a strong plot in mind and develop it using your characters? Those are two approaches to writing," she smiled. "Which is yours?"

My mind whirled. What if I said the wrong thing? But I could only say what I did whether it was right or wrong. I thought of Michael and Merry, of the Kilts stories, the people in the plays I had done for Marguerite Puttick, and I said the only words I could say. "I get to know my characters so well that the action is theirs. I don't know anything about plot."

The smile that then spread over her face was like the sun rising. "That's the way I work."

My next call was on Lillian Bragdon, juvenile editor at Knopf. She asked me how soon I could follow *Quest in the Northland* with more adventures of the Lamb children.

May 10, 1940

The world news is shattering. Hitler has invaded France. There are bombings, bloodshed, and stricken people. Under Churchill, Britain is doing her mightiest to rearm, to deal with the blows as they come.

July, 1940

Mr. Bishop had yet another house to show us. It was a long drive to see it and through a part of the country new to us. Passing a group of shacks with every evidence of haphazard living, Mr. Bishop waved his hand and said, "These will all be cleaned out soon." Always he wanted us to see only the best. A wrath rose in me that I managed to stifle. But these are homes, people live in them, I thought to myself.

The house he took us to was not for us, but the sight of the shacks and the airy promise of demolition lodged in my mind. I didn't know what I could do about them, or about the social conditions that caused them, but maybe someday there would be something.

December, 1940

Between Christmas and New Year's we went to Boston. One night at a gathering of friends we met

Holden Greene, a contractor who had done much of the work at Sturbridge Village and who had a feeling for old houses. He and Bill spent most of the time talking together, and as we left Holden said, "When you find that house you're seeking, let me know. I'd like to have a hand in restoring it."

"I think things are going to happen soon," Bill said to me.

January, 1941

And they did!

Mr. Bishop phoned early of a cold bright day saying that he had a house he very much wanted to show us. It was not on the market, but he had been in touch with the owner, a farmer who lived near, to see if he would be willing to sell it. The farmer was. Enumerating its features, Mr. Bishop made it sound appealing—one of the first houses in Peterborough, 1789 the approximate date, on a black road, about a mile from the center, no plumbing, no electricity, but sound. "See for yourself."

It was so plain, and to me it was the least likely of all the houses we had seen. It had lost its small many-paned windows and had only long ones; there was a soapstone sink in the front room and water came in by gravity; the fireplaces had been boarded up. I couldn't see it, but Bill could. The more we talked and went through it room by room, the more certain Bill became that it was what we were seeking.

"It needs the touch of a master to restore it to its original state," Bill said, "and that is Holden Greene."

Then I yielded. We had not seen the house, though we must have passed by it many times, until after we met Holden Greene. The two went together.

When we told Mr. Bishop our search was over and the sooner we could have possession the better, he told us the price. "Five thousand dollars: house, barn, and outbuildings, sixty-seven acres of field and woods, a brook; but you will have to do a good deal to it to bring it up to present-day living."

That night we opened Father's envelope. In it was a letter: ". . . when you find the house that you both like, I will send you five thousand dollars as a down payment."

February, 1941

Events moved fast—the title search, the legalities, the deed, then Holden's survey of what the house needed, and the estimated cost. We secured an FHA loan from the bank and work commenced. Holden had two skilled carpenters who moved in with their camp beds as soon as the people who were renting the house moved out. What a story it was, I thought, everything coming together the way the parts of a book do, one event depending on another.

"Bill, remember Old Donal and what he said about a bargain and the worries being over?"

"I've thought of him often."

March, 1941

When the fireplaces were opened, one revealed the original hearth, built to the famous Rumford design; when the stairs were unsheathed, there was more light; when a dormer was cut into the roof, there was space for two bedrooms and a bath upstairs. Small-paned windows replaced the long ones. Plumbing, heating, and electricity were installed under the watchful eye of Holden Greene. If a hinge needed to be replaced, or even a mantel, he found one that was of the period. Always he knew what should be done to preserve the old, to blend it with the new, and his men worked as if the house were their own.

The earth floor in the summer kitchen which would be our dining room was laid with wide pine boards. The buttery became a modern kitchen. Bill and I helped where we could, stripping layers of paint from paneling to get down to the plain pine, and some of the boards were twenty-two inches wide. The most thrilling moment was when layers of wallpaper came off the room that would be our guest room, beneath them was stenciling. "Done about 1815," Holden said, "By a journeyman stenciler, and done for a bride, or those little hearts would never have been part of the design."

There were days when too much was going on for us to be of any use, so we took time off to explore. The sun was riding high and melting the snow. We could begin to plan where our garden would be. We went to the woods and discovered the brook, the old sugar house, the great trees, the stone walls, the magnificent boulders.

May, 1941

The house was ready for painting. The shutters, which were now in place, gave it the look it must have had in its early days. I imagined a red house, or perhaps a yellow one with gray trim.

Holden was shocked. "But this is an old house. It must be what it always was. White. The best color in this countryside. With dark, very dark, green shutters."

I bowed to the man whose feeling for tradition was so strong and right.

There came a day when the work was finished, even the clearing up. The two workmen invited us to supper, laying a plank over two sawhorses for a table in what would be our living room and drawing up nail kegs to sit on. Color came in the soft green of the walls, the brick of the fireplace, and one red rose the men had put in a milk bottle on the table. The next morning they packed up and were gone.

During the past years Bill and I had lived in lovely places—Wythburn Court, Heimeli, White House, Edwardes Square, and others of lesser duration, but now we were home. We had our shieling, our own croft. When our furniture arrived it would bring something of England to New England. We had had goals through the years and now we had a major one: to be settled by Memorial Day weekend when Mother and Father were coming to be our first guests in the room with the stenciled walls.

They liked the house, feeling that it was the perfect place for Bill and me.

"It's well built," Father said.

"It's friendly," Mother added.

They sensed, as we had, that part of its charm was the way the past lay so lightly upon it. There were no creaking floors, no hint of the supernatural. It had been the home of simple, hard-working farming folk over close to two centuries. We were only the fifth in its line of owners, and we felt we would be true to its tradition.

Mother and Father were accompanied by a young, sleek Scottish terrier whose name was Bonnibel. "We knew you shouldn't be without a dog," Father said as he handed me her AKC papers. Again a canny Scot would have a part in our lives!

July, 1941

There had been little time for writing, but I knew that I must soon establish a routine, and it was Bill who was giving me a gift of time as he took on many household tasks. He brought in the wood, laid the fires, dried the dishes, and never did one slip from his fingers. When it came to housecleaning, he claimed the floors and the porcelain in the bathrooms as his right. In the garden, weeding between the rows and thinning were his specialties. His fingers had a sensitivity that served him well now that he had started to learn braille.

The books were bringing in royalties, even from war-ravaged England, and their numbers were increasing. The Lambs had more adventures in a book called *Haven for the Brave.* A collection of children's stories, written over the years, among them *The Marriage Tapestries* which grew as I worked on the needlepoint seats for our dining room chairs, had been gathered into a book: *Under the Little Fir.* I sent it to several publishers, finally approaching John Day because of *Piskey Folk.* It was not for them, but they suggested their associate firm, Coward-McCann. Rose Dobbs, the juvenile editor, and I seemed to see alike about the book. When I mentioned having the artwork done by Nora Unwin, she agreed, "If she can get the work done under wartime conditions." Nora could and did and, to me, the illustrations far outshone the text. John Day was doing one of the Tregarthen stories found in the old trunk, *The Doll Who Came Alive,* and Nora's drawings gave it zest.

Lillian had had enough of the Lambs and asked me to be open to a wholly new idea. I soon discovered it was very near. Out of the house itself came something I longed to write. The stenciled walls began to speak in a language I understood. I found myself going about the pattern of my days—the simple chores of the house, the reading aloud to Bill, the trips in to town, the walks with Bonnie—while another pattern was weaving itself in my mind; the people began to become more real than those I met in the course of a day.

September, 1941

Shieling, our shelter, had become a shelter for Ann, our old friend from Boston. She had been so good to us, and now she had need of the kind of counsel that Bill was deft at giving. She settled into the guest room and was glad to help around and about, but most of her time was spent with Bill. Aside from getting the meals, I was able to be for longer periods of time at my desk in the room that looked out on mountains.

October, 1941

Out of the past came the villain I needed, and what story was ever without a villain? The villain was the weather of 1816, weather that caused the year to be known in the annals of New Hampshire as eighteen hundred and froze-to-death. I went to the State Library at Concord for books of the period. I read newspapers so old they all but crumbled in my hands. The Farmer's Almanac of the time gave me facts I needed for the year that caused havoc for most people, but that made Jared

111

Austin. As soon as I had the journeyman stenciler named, he became real to me, as did Jennet and Mr. Toppan, Corban Cristy, the Dunklees, and all the rest.

November 3, 1941

The idea seems so wonderful that I tremble before it. Way down deep inside me is a feeling that I can never do justice to it, then I remember that I have felt this way before, and it is just the prick I need. But still I am waiting for something. I see parts of the story, but it has not come together as a whole.

November 13, 1941

At supper tonight Ann and Bill were talking together, and suddenly the whole structure of the story became clear to me—a house that had been framework became habitable, ready to be moved into. As I followed events in my mind, I felt in a different world, not knowing or even hearing what Ann and Bill were saying to each other. I wanted to shout for joy, and yet I wanted to keep it close to myself until I got a net of words around the idea.

November 14, 1941

This day actual writing begins. I make a rough plan and start the first chapter. I wonder how long it will be and then realize that it will be exactly as long as it must be for the story. It will tell me as it unfolds; it is not for me to dictate to it. Beauty Is a Bright Flame *is my working title.*

November 21, 1941

First chapter is done and the outline of the whole is shaping up well. Jared has acquired his own character and is taking things into his own hands.

112

December 3, 1941

I've lingered some days over some reading that has just come to light. It is helping me with the background. Now I begin the second chapter.

December 7, 1941

The United States has entered the war. Pearl Harbor has been bombed with frightful destruction and loss of life. My heart has been so torn for England and the long-loved friends; now I feel closer to them, and somehow the suffering is easier to bear, as we are all in it together. I work harder than ever today. Holding on to something good and beautiful is a line of life.

December 11, 1941

Well launched now, but the waters are deep, and I'm rowing hard. Soon the current will carry me.

December 12, 1941

A letter from Lillian today, "Hoping to get your new manuscript before too long." Three chapters are done.

December 19, 1941

Finished chapter four. Halfway mark, I think.

December 29, 1941

Took time out for Christmas, but glad to be back at my desk with Jared wending his way to New Hampshire. The real part of the story is opening up.

113

January 14, 1942

On chapter seven now, with the excitement mounting. The end begins to be in sight. I love it and feel a day ill spent if there has been no converse with Jared.

January 15, 1942

Lillian wants the manuscript as soon as possible. I think I'll be done in ten days, then for the hard but gratifying part—revision and correction.

January 18, 1942

Nearing fulfillment. Thrilled by it all.

January 23, 1942

DONE!

January 28, 1942

Read the first chapter aloud to Bill. He likes it. So do I. Commenced typing.

February 4, 1942

Only one chapter typed. It is slow going, but it does read well, and Bill continues to like it.

February 15, 1942

Half typed.

February 27, 1942

Finished and off to Knopf. I feel like a mother whose child has put on long trousers and gone away to school. It's not mine any more.

March 12, 1942

Lillian says there is not a word that doesn't ring true. She gives it the title Patterns on the Wall. Of course, that is exactly what it is. Now for the long wait for production. Lillian says it will be published in the spring of 1943.

May 10, 1942

One of the small joys is writing essays to go with Bill's pictures. With them we can relive the weekend walks we had, the travels we made, the climbs, the places seen, the people. I'm glad for that clutch of little notebooks, for I always carried one in pocket or rucksack. Bill helps me in remembering. His sense for detail is sharp. There have been no pictures now for some time, but Bill still loves to fondle his Leica. Next to me, he says, it is his dearest possession; but he has made up his mind to part with it. Tomorrow when we go to Boston he is determined to sell it.

May 12, 1942

Bill says it is time I have a new typewriter and so he has got one for me.

June 21, 1942

Rose Dobbs has come for a few days and we talk about a book I am planning. It is based on a true happening. A woman, in our

*neighboring town of Temple, nursed a stillborn lamb to life. The
lamb grew to be a member of the family and the leader of the flock.*

*"Yes, it can be a good story," Rose agreed. "When will you
have it for me?"*

*"Soon, but it may take a while for Nora to do the illustrations
as things are now."*

"Do you have a title?"

"Mountain Born."

*We talked much more, of course, but it is thrilling to tell an
editor about an idea and then be told to go ahead.*

October 5, 1942

*Now Lillian has just gone after being here three days. She
brought the galleys of* Patterns *for me to read and return to her.
It is with awe that I see my words in type. They look so important,
and only a year ago they were tumbling around in my head. She
said they were coming out with an extra page and did I want a
dedication. I do:* "To my Mother, with love and gratitude."

1943–1945

PATTERNS ON THE WALL

Winter, *1943*

Perhaps we had been readying ourselves, Bill more consciously than I, but on that bitter day when I took him down to Boston for the operation that might preserve some sight, I still hoped. Two weeks later, when we drove back to Shieling, Bill was a man who would not see again. The optic nerves had been severed and the eyes had been removed. "He will have no more pain," the doctor said. Plastic eyes, gray as his own had been, now confronted the world. The doctor said many helpful things to me, but more than all the practical things were the words, "Keep him seeing." He had been amazed that Bill had done as much as he had, got on as well as he had, during the past year.

That Bill had been able to do so much was due in large part to the way he had learned to see intently because of his photography. Composition, focus, quality of light, all that made him skilled in his craft, had built into him some power that helped him to go on seeing. But, persistent in hope as I had been, something had been preparing me, too. Memory bore me back to that last day at Oaksmere when Mrs. Merrill took the seniors to a vaudeville show and one of the acts had been a blind comedian who sang a song with the refrain:

> My darling, my wife, the light of my
> life,
> Has eyes that can see for me.

I did not know Bill then, and I certainly knew little about blindness except as a word that indicated misfortune.

Bill was fifty-five, more than a midpoint in life and a point at which many might have given up; but not Bill. To him, losing his sight was another challenge, another beginning. It might take time, but finding a home took time. Finding what he could do might take a little longer.

His pictures were coming into use. The Icelandic ones were made into slides and put in order. Bill gave talks on Iceland to church groups, service clubs, and schools. Few people have been there, and little is known about the land that has such contrasts, such interesting people, and such inspiring history. I worked the projector and whispered the number of the slide coming up. Bill's memory had always been exceptional —lack of sight made it more so, and he had always been a good storyteller. The Skye pictures would come next as slides, then Cornwall, and with those we would be able to talk about the Tregarthen books and introduce them to people.

March, 1943

Rose Dobbs's interest in the story I told her about the lamb gave me all I needed to start writing, and now pages were piling up on my desk. Several strands, in addition to the tale of the lamb, came together to make the book. One was the longing to own a farm, perhaps a sheep farm, that Bill and I had for years. Another was the sweater a friend made for me from wool spun as it came from the sheep. It had a rich, oily smell and was full of twigs and burrs picked up while the sheep was grazing. I had only to bury my nose in it to feel like a sheep. Most important were the long talks I had with Sydney Stearns in Hancock, who had five hundred sheep in his care. After every story he told me, he added, "Sheep are very intelligent creatures."

I sent to Washington for Government pamphlets on sheep raising, the needs, problems, diseases, rewards. I felt I had to know all those things even though I might use only a small part in the actual book. I went over to Temple to talk with Mrs. Leighton. During my first call, when we were sitting in the kitchen with cups of coffee, I heard a sharp clicking sound as if someone wearing high heels were coming to join us. Someone was—the lamb-grown-sheep, Flickertail. That was what Winnie Leighton called her when she saw the motion of tail that gave evidence of life.

Ten years had gone by, and Flickertail was as much a part of the household as a dog. She went to Grange meetings with the Leightons, even to church, waiting outside. Everyone in the town knew her and, when I got her story written, many more people would know her. In the book her name was Biddy.

When my pages were written, a copy went to Nora in England, for she was working on the illustrations. Fortunately, her war service put her in a home, helping to care for children, instead of in a factory making munitions, so she could get on with her work as she had time available. If the artwork was not delayed and if it all reached New York safely, Rose hoped to have the book ready by the end of the year. It was hard to do, mainly because I had to allow for interruptions in my time, but I gave it my best. However, I can never be really sure until I have a word of "Well done" from the publisher, the editor in this case.

It came, and I was gratified.

April 5, 1943

This day Patterns on the Wall *is published. I hold it in my hands. It has been given a beautiful format. Warren Chappell's decorations are so exactly right. Tonight I shall start reading it aloud to Bill.*

May, 1943

We had been on the "Home Front" ever since the United States entered the war, and so were better able to bear the news of human suffering and material destruction because we were involved and everyone was doing something to help. My time away from Shieling was limited, as there was so much I could do for Bill, but one task I could fulfill was that of plane spotter at the Post on the slope of East Pack, only a few miles from Shieling. Volunteers were instructed in the different types of planes "the enemy" used and we knew how to report them if seen or heard. The observation place was a small hut, manned by two spotters in shifts around the clock. One pair of eyes must always be on the sky, one pair of ears equally alert, especially when clouds rolled down the mountain. We had a telephone to report anything questionable. I was at the Post several afternoons a week. There was no chance to read or write, or even talk, but I could think while my eyes were on the sky and I was already working, in my mind, on a novel.

One day the telephone rang. My companion and I looked at each other in horror and bewilderment. It could only be a ghastly emergency. As I was near the phone, I answered.

"Air Spotter Detail, East Pack Mountain," I said.

A familiar ripple of laughter came over the wire. "I may be court-martialed for doing this, but I had to let you know—you've had a telegram from New York. *Patterns* has just been given the *Herald Tribune* Spring Festival Award." The receiver clicked.

"*Patterns*—" Suddenly I was unloosed. I put my head in my hands and cried.

My companion rushed over to me. "Where are the planes? Is New York being bombed? Washington?"

I shook my head and tried to explain, but it was hard to get her to understand the importance of the news to me.

There was another telephone call that night from Lillian with all the details. "The award is to be presented at the *Herald Tribune* office on Friday. You must be here."

I knew that I could not be. There was a commitment to the Air Spotter Post, but more than that, Bill needed me. I told Lillian that I could not be there, but that my mother happened to be in New York, staying at the Commodore, and that I would ask her to accept the award for me.

Mother telephoned to say how proud she was to accept the award—a check for two hundred dollars. "The judges said the book merited the award for its

121

beauty and its order." How astonishingly right this all was—that Mother should be the one to hear those words about my book, to be a part of the joy and the triumph.

Summer, 1943

The crabapple tree on the south side of the house has long been a part of the life here. When we first saw it, the bare branches against a snowy landscape made it look like a dancer, reaching up, bending but not bowing. When it blossomed, it made us want to bow to its beauty, and when it bore fruit we had to bow many times to fill our baskets with small yellow apples with their pink blush. We made jelly, even tried wine, and gave much of the crop away. Bill had asked me about the tree, and, because I wanted him to *see* it this of all years, I wrote a poem about it.

> The house had just been built
> the year I first bore fruit—
> apples with which a child played
> in thin September shade.
> Cold strengthened me and when
> spring came round again
> white blossoms crowned my head.
> "Look!" the little girl cried,
> "our tiny crab tree is a bride."
>
> When she wore bridal dress
> I had attained my height.
> A branch of mine could rest
> on the wall to the west;
> another reached to salute
> the east with ripening fruit.
> Baskets of apples I bore,

122

plenty rode my golden tide,
but with every spring I was a bride.

Families changed in the house
and my apples were used
for jelly and wine, sliced,
put into jars and spiced.
A nest rode me like an ark,
woodpeckers drilled my bark.
Years were so many leaves
tossed windward and wide,
but with every spring I was a bride.

Storms swept over my limbs,
ice bent my branches down,
but only the weight of my gold
ever broke a bough's hold.
Gnarled now and deep of root,
robust bearer of fruit,
I give shade, yield to wind,
stand breasting life's tide,
for with every spring I am a bride.

October, 1943

And now I held in my hands *Mountain Born.*

Nora's illustrations caught so wondrously the feeling and the beauty of the countryside in which the story was set, and yet she had never been in New Hampshire; but she did have Bill's photographs! Most wondrous of all is her depiction of Benj. When writing about him, I had in my mind's eye Mr. Hill, the farmer who, with his one old horse and mowing machine, had done our big field for the past two years. He was so calm, so peaceful, and did the work with a minimum of commotion and a maximum of effectiveness. Mr.

Hill might have posed for Nora, so precisely does he come out in her illustrations, and with him the philosophy of a man who has grown old and wise while working with animals and the land.

Winter, 1944

Rose asked me the question that I was beginning to learn is usual with editors, "What next?" I told her what was in my mind, a story that had been growing there for years and that is laid in England. "That sounds like a novel, and you will have to talk with Mr. Coward about it."

I could not possibly talk with Mr. Thomas R. Coward until I had something to show him, so I began to bring my thoughts together. Once the process was started, I was amazed at how much was there. The idea began for me that first year we were living in London, being a part of English life. Even though I often wanted to be taken as English, I was never more grateful that I was an American than when I became aware of social barriers, the class system that prevailed. My feeling was especially for the house servants, who worked for a pound a week and often less, and had little time for themselves. Granted they had their uniforms supplied, their meals provided and their rooms, those rooms were far from comfortable. Looking at houses that first year when we were renting furnished ones made this very clear to me, and the basement kitchens were often dismal except for the big coal range. From different maids we had—Maude, Elsie, Phyllis—hearing them tell of their own experiences, then getting them to have friends write down their experiences, I had plenty of material, some of it dating before the turn of the century; yet parallel with this was my deep love for England.

The story of Susie Minton, who went into service at the age of thirteen in 1883 because it was the "respectable" and often the only work for a girl, came into being for me against the background of London and the English countryside. Writing the story, I felt that I was repaying a debt to England while revealing something that troubled me. When I started to write, the story flowed easily, for I had so much material at hand and there were memories that were very fresh. My manuscript was about finished when I met an English woman and her daughter, the Buchanans, who were teaching in a school in Connecticut. They came to stay at Shieling for a week, and Mrs. Buchanan read my work line by line, word by word, checking, correcting, even approving. When I had typed *Wind of Spring,* I felt ready to submit it to Mr. Coward.

June, 1944

Something about Susie Minton must have touched his heart, or perhaps Rose put in a good word for me, since *Mountain Born* was doing nicely, because Mr. Coward was not long in accepting *Wind* just as it was. He suggested no change in my title, though he agreed that one might have to read the book to discover what it meant. It came from those lines of Thomas Moore's that foresee changes coming in the social structure:

> Then shall the reign of mind
> commence on earth
> And starting fresh as from a second
> birth,

Man in the sunshine of the world's
     new spring
Shall walk transparent like some holy
     thing.

The day I signed the contract in his office, I could not have asked for any greater praise: "You know what you're talking about." He smiled, that shy smile that people saw rarely. "Now, see if you can find something nearer home."

There was something in my mind that went back to the time when Mr. Bishop was showing us the countryside, wanting us to see only what was attractive. I realized later that he often went out of his way to avoid the unattractive, like the day when he went by some tumbledown shacks and with a wave of his hand said they would all be cleaned out soon. Something in me rose up in rebellion. These are homes where people live, I wanted to shout, but I didn't say anything. Some people can let their fury out in spoken words and get it over with. I'm not like that. With me it goes deep into mind and, often, heart and then comes out gradually in written words.

Mr. Coward had stirred up something in me, but I had a lot of thinking to do.

October, 1944

Things began to come together and, as so often, in unexpected ways.

When Bill and I were on our way home from Boston one day, we gave a ride to a young sailor. I stopped at the post office to pick up our mail, and the sailor asked Bill, "Is she a teacher? She walks like one."

Several times last winter I was asked by Marion Hudson, a friend who is a teacher at Keene State College, to talk with her class about children's literature in general and my books in particular. One of Marion's students is now the teacher in a one-room school in a small village a few miles north of Keene. I spent a day with Evelyn Osborn, sitting in the back of the room, and the children thought no more of me than of a piece of furniture. There were seventeen children in six grades, and I was fascinated as I watched how Evelyn led them in what, at their different stages of development, they were capable of doing, drawing out the best, encouraging, loving, disciplining. I made many more visits, listening, observing, writing down what I heard and saw in my notebook.

The school itself, the village, the tar-paper shacks on the edge of the woods from which two of the children came, the people, some so kind, some so unkind, began to give me what I needed. Soon the children accepted me as part of a day, and they began to share themselves with me. Evelyn let me in on a wonderful secret: that the children had asked if I could be the one to present the diplomas when graduation time came in June. Two boys and a girl were graduating and would be going on to high school in Keene.

Bit by bit the story began to weave itself into a fabric in my mind, from the notes I had been making during my visits to that one-room school. I began to feel that Mr. Coward might realize that it was nearer home, so near that suddenly I found myself with a title, *Nearby*, before even a word had been written or a plan made.

This morning when I went out to the mailbox I found a package—it is my copy of Wind of Spring, *and with it a letter from Mr. Coward. He says it has already been bought for publication in England. "Not a large sum, but at least it moves your name into a rising rank of writers who are concerned about how 'the other half lives.'"*

It is a small thin book with a notice in the front saying:

> IMPORTANT:
> *Government wartime restrictions on materials have made it essential that the amount of paper used in each book be reduced to a minimum. This volume is printed on lighter paper than would have been used before material limitations became necessary, and the number of words on each page has been substantially increased. The smaller bulk in no way indicates that the text has been shortened.*

On the facing page there were just two words that really mattered: "To William." We started to read it that night. Bill didn't want me to stop.

February, 1945

Bonnibel was becoming an important part of the life at Shieling, for she was bred to one of Mrs. John Winant's best dogs. This meant several trips to Concord, the state capital, just an hour's drive away. We even went to the State House to meet Governor Winant. While in his office, we were introduced to Mr. Herbert Rainie, apparently a distinguished lawyer. He told Bill of an organization, the New Hampshire Association for the Blind, and said that he was serving as president. In a gruff but kindly way, he added that he would like to come to Peterborough and talk with Bill sometime. He seemed particularly interested that Bill had been learning to read and write braille.

"That's hard work for anyone, but at your age—why do you do it?"

Bill's answer was, "What's the alternative?"

March, 1945

My story of the schoolteacher was quickening in me and I was glad for mornings when I could work without interruptions. I sat at my desk, my jam jar full of sharpened pencils, and contemplated those long yellow legal pages of my pad, blank but soon to be filled with words. I suppose I could write directly on the typewriter, but writing is a craft, and, to me, seeing the words come from my hand onto the paper means a closer connection with my mind and my heart. It's slow, of course, but for me it is the way. The value of the legal pads is that the number of written words on one is close to the number of typed words on an 8 1/2-by-11-inch sheet.

I began writing. Thinking and planning had gone on for so long that I knew my setting and had named my people. Now I could really get going. The first day was slow and halting, but sure. People and situations came to me as if out of a mist. I had to take time to see them clearly.

The story gained momentum so rapidly that I wanted to stay with it all the time. I was writing something like twenty-five hundred words a day—a morning, that is. I stopped at noon. There were other things to be done: meals to get, household tasks, people to see.

129

April, 1945

There were several demands and I had to be away from my desk for almost three weeks. I picked up the threads and found to my joy that the story itself was carrying me forward. Nothing was lost, perhaps it was even better for having been set aside for a while.

June, 1945

If I can keep my time free, I should be finished by the end of July, then I'll put the manuscript away for two months before I start revision and the final typing.

September, 1945

It did not get finished in July, because such a wonderful opportunity came for Bill. He was asked to go for the school year to Perkins Institution for the Blind in Watertown, just outside Boston. He is to teach business organization, selling techniques, and consumer education and, in return, be taught advanced braille, typing, and woodworking. What an exchange: Bill's thirty years of business experience balanced by the gaining of skills that a blind person needs to get on in life! That chance meeting with Mr. Rainie last winter was what set this all in motion. We were busy getting Bill's things ready. I took him to Perkins and helped him get settled. He would be home weekends, but during the week I would have hours and hours for work, and the story should surge along.

When I got to my desk and confronted all those pages, I had forgotten that I had gone so far. It took me a long time to read up to page 307. It must be good, I thought, for so much of it gives me shivers. When I came to page 308 and it was blank, I could hardly bear it. I prayed, "Heaven help me: what I want to say is so big, can I possibly get it into words?"

In eight days chapter ten was finished, but I had a long way still to go. This book was showing me more than any of the others that I don't invent my characters, I entertain them. Mary Rowen, the teacher, had been close to me from the start, but when Dan first came into my ken it was quite different. He seemed to emerge from the woods, came across the stone wall, over the field, and then into my room. But I saw him only hazily at first, and he was so shy. It was days before I could get him to sit down and really talk with me.

November, 1945

At 7 P.M. November 1 and at the end of a radiant day, the last words were written, and I printed at the bottom of the page "EBENEZER—Hitherto hath the Lord helped me." That was what George Eliot wrote when she had finished a book. I sent Bill a telegram that would be read to him: "Dan got married last night. Expects to live happily ever after."

November 6, 1945

How is it that twelve red roses can say more than any words, especially when we are away from each other?

This year has held many marvels—for the world, cessation of the war; for us, events that enrich our lives. The only way I can bring it to a fitting conclusion is by quoting George MacDonald in a letter to a friend: "I do not myself believe in misfortune, anything to which men give the name is merely the shadow-side of a good."

1946

BONNIBEL'S FAMILY

The great event we now looked forward to was Nora's coming to stay with us for a year! We had accomplished so much with books against tumult and distance, that to think of being able to work together, with her at Shieling, filled me with happiness. Exit permits and visas were hard to obtain, as restrictions on travel had not lessened with peace, and there seemed to be endless details to arrange. Bill appealed to Governor Winant and he was so helpful. The way was now finally clear. Nora had her exit permit, her visa, and her flight on British Airways for sometime in April. That was as definite as anything could be and more than anything had been.

It was Bonnibel who began all this, for it was her relationship to a Winant dog that began our friendship with the Winants and so enlisted the Governor to do what he could in Nora's case. Bonnie's first puppies were both so fine, two males, and they went to Mrs. Winant as part of our understanding. Bonnie would be bred again and this time we would have first choice.

133

So we looked ahead. The best thing to do on the first month of a new year. I knew how important it was for Bill to have something always ahead. It might be just going out to dinner the next week, but a date on his calendar meant anticipation, and that meant something good was before us.

Bill went back to Perkins, and I had to work hard with this stretch of alone time. I finished revising *Nearby* and started typing, setting myself a stint of ten pages a day.

February 20, 1946

It's 5 P.M. and the final page is typed. Now to wrap it up in a neat package and send it on its way to New York. How long must I wait before I get a word of "Well done." A whisper would satisfy me, though I would like a shout.

March 16, 1946

Today a telegram came: BOOK IS FINE.

March, 1946

I made a quick trip to New York. In Mr. Coward's office I basked—not in sunshine, but in the warmth of his praise. He showed me the jacket for the book— already done! I liked it. He told me of plans he had for English publication, submission to a book club, when publication would be, the few changes they would like me to make "if you agree." If I agree! When have I not been grateful to an editor for seeing something that my eyes and mind had missed? The changes were so slight that I made them that night at the hotel. His words were never many, but he said four to me that I shall hold on to: "Stick to your last." He handed me an envelope and said it was an advance against royalties. I didn't open it in front of him, but when I did, I gasped —$750! He really must believe in the book. So did I, but then I had ever since the idea first took hold of me.

April, 1946

A letter came from Bill April 1, the first in a long time. He was not finding typing easy, so he wrote it in pencil on paper that rested on a pad with raised lines which he could feel. He hoped I could read it, and I could, even though he sometimes went over a line already written and sometimes went off the right edge. I copied it in my notebook for easier reading. If he gets to writing a book someday, he might want to have it to refer to. He said he had been remembering something he saw when he was staying at the farm in Kent while I was in Zurich:

I had gone to bed early and was lying wide awake, listening to the stillness and slowly sensing the fragrance of garden and meadow. Then I became aware of a pale panel of light on the wall; curving across the light were a few faint lines of shadow. And even as I realized that the lights of a car coming down the Old Mill road were shining through the branches of a tree standing near my window, the patch grew brighter and the shadows darker and sharper.

There, on this canvas of yellow light, were three slender branches lifting themselves into the picture from the wide frame of darkness. From each branch, tender young twigs

135

shot off to right and left and from them fat buds curved to a quick point. I thought how like a lovely Chinese painting, with its delicate feeling created by a few swift strokes.

Then a night breeze must have stirred the tree outside, for the shadows began to move gently to and fro across the panel. I was fascinated by the effect and had begun to fit a silent tune to their rhythmic dance when of a sudden, like a Cinderella at the stroke of twelve, they raced across the square of light— and disappeared. The room was again in darkness. I heard the motorcar going up the road toward the village.

It is an answer to the question I was often asked, "But how does Bill see so much?" It isn't *how,* but *what.* His sight might be restricted, but his vision had no limits.

Remembering when we saw holly that first Christmas in Devon—the prickly leaves within reach, the smoother leaves and great bunches of berries so beyond reach—I wrote a poem about it. I planned to send it to Bill, but as I had not mastered braille, someone would have to read it to him.

The Holly Speaks

O holly, your berries red
are so high above my head!
Out of my reach, yes quite,
and so temptingly bright!
Jewels set in wintry skies,
but only for my eyes.
O holly, have you no words?
"Yes, I must remember
my birds."

O holly, your leaves prick
my fingers when I pick
even one branch, but if I
could only reach up high,
I'd have berries, boughs and all.
Not a prickle however small
is on those branches, but leaves
smooth turned in glistening sheaves.
O holly, have you no words?
        "Yes, I must remember
                my birds."

Those hard fruits the birds will shun,
They'll not have them, no not one!
        "No, not now while there's
                food,
            but should the winter brood
            and the earth freeze to stone
            and the hips be all gone,
            the birds will flock round
            that which hardness has kept
                sound."

Bitter as wind from the east,
can the birds call that a feast?
        "Feasts are made of answered
                needs.
            Forgetting for what it pleads,
            a bird is happy to dine
            on such berries as mine
            from a table of green
            by the wind swept clean.
            What matter bitter with
                sweet to follow,
            Spring on the wing of a
                swallow?

Spring at the forest's foot,
a-stir in each primrose root?"

O holly, I love your words!
    "Yes, I must remember
        my birds."

April 18 was a day to mark with a white stone—
Lewis Carroll's words for any day special beyond all
others. At last, after delays and many setbacks, Nora
arrived. In these postwar days, flights were so uncertain
and so often deferred that a saying was rife, "If you
have time to spare, go by air." But she was here; that
was what mattered.

I went to New York to meet her. Coming back on
the train, we talked so much that we were both hoarse
by the time we got to Boston, but there was so much
to say, so much to get caught up on. Bill was waiting
at Shieling to greet us, as it was his Easter vacation, and
we would all have several days together. Nora would
be part of our life now, part of the family of Shieling.
The visa said for a year, but we knew in our hearts that
it would be for much longer.

June, 1946

Rose Dobbs was here for two days to make plans
for the Christmas book that would involve both Nora
and me. Almost before illustrations and text were put
together, we knew to whom it would be dedicated—
Bertha Mahoney Miller; her inspiration and encourage-
ment were unfailing. Rose wrote in our guest book:

Come up here, O dusty feet!
Here is fairy bread to eat.

July, 1946

Bertha and William Miller came to tea one Sunday afternoon. I think tea, with thin slices of buttered bread and little cakes, is the meal I like best of all. The mahogany table in the dining room looked so lovely with a bowl of flowers from the garden, the Crown Derby, and the silver tea set. The Millers had a special something to ask Bill and that was that he go on the board of *The Horn Book* magazine. An honor, yes, but what an opportunity for him to put his business skills at the service of others!

Before they left, and as we were standing by the gate, Bertha said in her little quavery voice, "Are we just too old for you to call us by our first names?" We had always been formal with them, but what a question! Bill knew what to do. He took a step toward them, held out both hands, and in ringing tones called each one in turn and forever, "Bertha! William!"

Later, when we were in the kitchen doing the dishes, it brought tears to my heart to see the way Bill handled the Crown Derby teacups and saucers and plates. Phyllis used to say of him, "He is such a gentle man." That gentleness encompassed china as it did people; now it would be felt in editorial decisions.

End of Summer, 1946

Life was humming for us all. The garden was flourishing, both vegetables and flowers. I was able to establish a routine of work. Most mornings during the week I could be at my desk from after breakfast until luncheon. Nora worked busily at her drawing board in her bedroom studio, for many commissions came to her from other publishers, now that she was at hand, and Bill had his projects; then the afternoons were for chores and fun. How good it was to have Bill home! I depended on his help in the house, in the garden, in the woods where we were clearing trails. Bonnibel had her second family, a little female, which we would keep, and two little males, which would go to Mrs. Winant.

And there were guests, flowing through the house and through the summer. The most exciting was Alton Hall Blackington, Blackie to his radio audience. He had a program called *Yankee Yarns,* and he liked to get hold of anything that would make a good yarn. My use of the summer of eighteen hundred and froze-to-death was such a yarn. He and his wife came to stay with us so they could see the patterns on the wall in the guest room and talk with us at length about the stencils, the weather, the research. A few weeks later we heard ourselves on his program.

Nora completed the drawings for another of the Tregarthen stories, *The White Ring,* and was working on illustrations for *Once in the Year,* the book of mine that carries the people of *Mountain Born* into the Christmas season. Now she and Bill were planning a story of Bill's, *Andy, the Musical Ant.* It began when Nora and Bill started to make music together in their odd moments, playing recorders. It grew when Bill had occasion to make up a story for some children who were visiting us, and the story was about an ant who did not play a recorder but an accordion. When I typed the story so it could be sent to a publisher, I felt that the keys on my machine would burst out laughing.

Nora had a marvelous time getting her sketches,

crawling around the field and lying on her back under a goldenrod to get an ant's eye view of the world, studying an anthill, then getting the sort of book from the library that showed what an anthill was like on the inside. She described everything to Bill with such care that his laughter rippled through the summer days. The story grew from a jingle of Bill's about ants as they went about their busyness:

> Work, work,
> There's nothing else worthwhile;
> Work, work,
> Don't even stop to smile.

But Andy had a different idea, and work was not for him as he went around with his accordion:

> Play, play,
> All work is bad for one;
> Play, play,
> An ant must have some fun.

The anthill, faced by catastrophe, was saved by Andy's playing, so the National Anthem became:

> Work, play,
> For each is well worthwhile;
> Play, work,
> Be sure you stop to smile.

Now of course, we have an unwritten rule at Shieling that no ant must ever be disturbed, no matter what his business in flower or vegetable garden, because it just might be Andy; and an anthill was to be respected.

We sent the story and roughs of the illustrations to Lillian. It did not take her long to say that this would be for her and that next time she came to Shieling she would talk seriously about it with both Bill and Nora.

Reading galley proof on *Nearby* was taking some of my time, and I had the perfect system. I read for two hours, then went out to the garden to weed or hoe for two hours, then back to my desk. The tasks complemented each other, and one made the other easier.

There is another side to writing a book and that is the letters that come because of the book. The mail brought many from children who have read *Mountain Born* and liked it and wanted to be sure that I would write back to them. Sometimes their letters had such similarity that I suspect they had been told in a school class "to write to an author." One writer was honest enough to say, "If you answer this letter, I'll get an extra mark." Most of the time the letters were spontaneous and the children expressed themselves in charming ways. One such writer said, "I liked it all, except the end when it leaves you just sitting there wondering if there's any more." And there was the occasional child who more than anything wanted to have a pen pal. "Will you be mine?" The letters from people who read *Wind of Spring* were thoughtful, and those who wrote about *Patterns on the Wall* had a glow to them. Not yet had I had a negative letter. Perhaps only people who like books take time to write to the authors.

I do answer the letters, but in such a way that it will not encourage correspondence. I used to be amused when I heard a person talk about having to save herself for something. I was finding that I did have to save myself for the stories I wanted to write, the ideas I wanted to explore. Much as I have loved during the years to write letters to my friends, I couldn't afford now to spend myself that way. My best thoughts would go into my books. Perhaps people would get used to finding them there.

November 10, 1946

Lillian has been here for three days. She came to go over the text and illustrations for Andy and to start planning the book, though she has no immediate publication in mind. She is no longer with Knopf, but with American Book Company, and the name for her department is Aladdin Books. This happens, she says. It seems to me that a writer is more closely linked with an editor than with a firm. Lillian is superb to work with, so is Rose. So soon they become friends more than editors. I put Mr. Coward in a slightly different category and am still a little in awe of him.

1947

BELOVED BONDAGE

January 6, 1947

What a way to start the year—*Nearby* was published today!

We had a Coming Out Party at the John Hancock House—we being all those who were involved in the book, and that is six: me, of course, and Bill for standing by and giving me courage and counsel, Marion Hudson for starting me off on the idea, Nora who did the sketch of me that is on the jacket. Percy Hudson and Dorris Frost, Marion's sister, were included because they knew about the book's coming into being, though they did not know the book until they saw it. Evelyn Osborn, on whom my Mary Rowen was patterned, should have been with us but she had some other commitment that night. She was there in spirit, and Marion will share it with her when next she sees her. What a party—place cards made by Nora, jingles composed by Bill, and a toast written by me! To honor Bill:

> With us tonight is one whose wisdom
> gleams

Like light from windows in kind
   golden streams,
And linking hands with wit his
   thoughts engage
The reader, flowing from page to
   page.
His was the steady hand, the mind's
   keen eye
That kept a level between earth and
   sky.
His was the voice that said, "Is this
   your best?
If it is not, then see you take no
   rest. . . ."

To honor Marion:

And there is one who, from the start,
Loved as her own and cherished in
   her heart. . . .
And from her fund of knowledge,
   from her store
Brought this and that to lift the book
   from lore
To actuality and sometime power.
This is the one who, in doubt's lone
   dark hour,
Gave courage to complete the work
   begun.

And Nora toasted me:

There is one here who saw a host of
   words
Reaching to heaven like a flight of
   birds.
She caught them in a net of love and
   care,

And nurtured them, then loosed them
to the air. . . .

The dinner was superb and everyone enjoyed everything, I especially. There was a time when Bill liked to analyze handwriting, and he was as much of a master as Old Donal was in reading tea leaves. Bill discovered something in my writing that indicated "likes to eat." Yes, I do, but more in savor than surfeit.

January 7, 1947

Shall I ever be able to get back to work?

January 14, 1947

Mr. Coward telephones to say that Nearby *has been accepted by the People's Book Club and that a check for $10,000 will shortly be coming to me.*
Oh!
What can I say? Thankfulness so immense spills over everything.

January, 1947

There was an idea growing in me. *Nearby* took time, five years really; and this would, too. It had to do with finding freedom within limitations. What started me was standing by the south window in the living room one morning and looking out at the snow whirling across the field. The wind was wild, free one might say. Before me on the table was a pot of white cyclamen, a dozen blooms, like white birds poised and resting, free in another way:

Beyond
was a flawless expanse of snow
from which slim trees rose dark and
    nude.
The wind swept high, the wind
    swung low,
ecstatic in its solitude.
Scattering drifts in rampaging delight,
the wind roared on in the path of the
    night.

Within
was a cyclamen full and white,
flowers poised like birds to wing a
    world,
buoyantly resting, gay and light.
The pot was only where roots lay
    curled
for the cyclamen was free. And the
    wind—
was it more so, being undisciplined?

It was a difficult idea, and it would be a long time before
I would be able to talk with Mr. Coward about it.

February 6, 1947

*Nearby's first printing, 7,500, went in a month and it is
now into a second. I am learning from the reviews. My heart warms
to the favorable ones; my mind quickens to the others. Yes, I can
see some of the faults in my writing: a tendency to preach, to drive
a moral too hard, to tell the reader what to think instead of making
a situation so clear that thinking is inevitable. All of this makes
me eager to get on to the next book, to see if I can overcome my faults.*

The letters were fabulous. One delighted me especially, "That title is wonderful—not only as applied to

living democracy but also in living the life that is nearby you now, and not waiting for the right time or better conditions. Just that one word means a tremendous amount." And the letters were coming from the most amazing people and places—from Mrs. Franklin Roosevelt, from the National Education Association, from radio stations asking how available I was for a program, and from teachers all over the country who felt the book spoke for them.

Of all the letters, the most exciting was the one that had the *big* check in it. Bill and I knew exactly what to do with it. We went to the bank and paid off the FHA loan on Shieling.

May, 1947

Mr. Rainie, the lawyer Bill had come to know in Concord, stopped by one afternoon on his way home from Boston. Blunt and always to the point, he wasted no time in telling Bill the purpose of his visit. I went to the kitchen to get tea and before I was back they had settled something. From then on there was nothing but pleasant chat. It wasn't until Mr. Rainie left that Bill told me what they had settled.

"The Directors of the New Hampshire Association for the Blind have decided that the organization should become more active. Mr. Rainie went down to Perkins to ask Dr. Farrell if he knew of anyone sympathetic to blindness, with some business experience, who might take on the work. Dr. Farrell said there was a man in their own backyard who could do it and he told Mr. Rainie about me."

"And you're going to do it?"

"Of course. There's a slight catch. He said I'd have

to find my own salary, that the funds were limited."

I had seen Bill face too many challenges not to realize that this to him was like the starting gun for a race.

We were soon asked to be present at a meeting of the board of the N.H.A.B. in Concord. Bill was told that they had voted to employ him as Executive Director, beginning September first. He would be the first paid employee the Association had ever had. He was allowed a budget of five thousand dollars for the first year, which was to include all travel and expenses, his own stipend, and the salary of a secretary. It was not unlike the arrangement I had entered into with A. and C. Black when I sold *High Holiday* outright. It had seemed then highly unbusinesslike; it soon proved otherwise.

Bill said as we were driving home, "It's a start. I have a chance to serve the blind, and my blindness is going to be my greatest asset."

August, 1947

Holden Greene came into our life again. As Nora's work expanded and her longer stay was an accepted fact, it was clear that she needed more than a bedroom-studio. Attached to the barn was a carriage shed, which had no other use than to hold wood, tools, and things that could easily be stored elsewhere. We saw it as a home for Nora. Holden studied it, made plans for it, and soon had his remarkable workmen on the job. The sills were sound, the uprights sturdy, and of the roof-beam Holden said, "You could hang a church on it."

In a few weeks, the shed was transformed into a dwelling for an artist. There was a fireplace, a tiny kitchen unit, a small room downstairs, and a large room with exposed beams upstairs, and all the facilities. Windows were long and wide, but many-paned, as they would have been in the old days. The view, more sweeping than that from the house itself, looked across barnyard and field to the East Mountains. There was a little porch made by extending the roof, and a flagged path that joined the Studio to Shieling. Holden had thought of everything—big shelves for art papers, drawers for tools, and the pegs that had been used to hold harnesses were soon holding easels and the pieces of equipment that were part of an artist's life. Linda, Bonnibel's daughter, had long ago attached herself to Nora. Now grown to a reliable age, she became Nora's companion. On the very day that the work was finished, Nora moved across the lawn with her books and papers, clothes, tools, work in progress, and Linda's basket.

Getting breakfast on Sunday morning had always been Nora's joyous rite. The kitchen was hers, and Bill and I did not appear until she called to us, and breakfast was always the same—cornbread and scrambled eggs, with the fruit that was at its best at the time; it might be raspberries from our own patch or blueberries from near hill slopes. This Sunday was no different. But even before the first cup of coffee was poured, Nora's Canticle of the Studio was read to us.

> Praise Thee, Lord, for Brother Studio,
> Who is so dear and friendly and
>   quiet.
> For the beauty of craftsmanship and
>   skill of mind
> That did fashion all his amenities—

And then it went on to praise Brother Barn and Sister Shieling, Fire and Wood and Stone and Mountain View and Little Lin. Everything was wrapped up in a paean of thanksgiving for

> Precious hours, long and quiet, spent
>   herein, with
> Rich reward of peace and joy and
>   creativity.

Breakfast itself, when it followed, was a long amen.

September, 1947

Bill was busy all summer making plans for his work. First was to find a secretary, a man who had bookkeeping and secretarial skills, who could drive, and who would be willing to turn himself to tasks around Shieling when a man's hand was needed. Bill would not have time now to carry on with many of the little chores that he had assumed as his. An ad in a Boston paper brought several responses, and one was exactly right, but he was not able to start until October. I did all I could that month to help Bill get going.

Office space was needed and for that, the guest room, with its patterns on the walls, answered. A card table, file boxes, and a braillewriter soon changed its appearance and limited us as to guests, but only for a while. Bill was already visualizing an office in Concord and much time traveling throughout the state. He had mastered braille to the extent that he made his own notes as I read him lists of cities, towns and their populations, and lists of names of people to be approached. Nora constructed for him a map of New Hampshire with raised lines for counties, raised dots for communities, and real humps for mountain ranges. Bill had a small stylus and pad that was pocket size, and at any time of day or night he could make notes and read them back.

Once he had familiarized himself with the state, he set about making a list of the people he wanted to call on. The lists were of men and women well known for their activities and for their financial support of good causes. First on the list was the name of a former governor, Huntley Spaulding, known for his stature and his generosity. Bill made constant use of the telephone, and his warm voice rippling over the wire said more, and more immediately, than the words of a letter. His intent was to make the work of the N.H.A.B. known, as well as its need for funds. When he phoned Governor Spaulding, he was invited to call the next week.

So we drove to Rye and called on Governor Spaulding. I was very much the background person and kept myself so, for, though I am Bill's wife, I am, in this instance, his driver and his secretary. I listened attentively to their conversation, but took no part in it. Bill had discovered some of Mr. Spaulding's interests and he spoke of them. They both talked about England and of baseball as compared with cricket. Quite casually Bill mentioned the work of the N.H.A.B., but he moved from it to other areas of interest and commented on the view of the ocean that was seen from the Spaulding house. Rye Beach is a lovely part of New Hampshire's brief coastline, and I had admired the expanse and described it to Bill as he and I walked up to the house.

We left after about an hour, and the two men

shook hands as if they had known each other for a much longer time. I was amazed that nothing, nothing whatever, had been said about money, and I thought that had been the purpose of our visit. Safely in the car and headed for home, I turned to Bill in exasperation.

"But, Bill, you never told him you needed funds to get the N.H.A.B. going."

"Of course not."

"But that was the whole point of our coming over."

He turned and looked at me. Schooled as I was to keep my eyes on the road ahead when driving, I turned only just enough to see the inscrutable look on his face and the smile behind it.

"You never talk about the money you want, you talk about other things."

"But I don't see—"

"You will."

October, 1947

T.K. had arrived and the first letter Bill dictated to him was one of thanks to Governor Spaulding for a very generous contribution to the work of the N.H.A.B. I learned my lesson.

Things happened rapidly. A small office was set up in Concord, and Bill was there three or four days every week. That ruled out the possibility of his having a Seeing Eye dog. Too much driving was necessitated and walking is requisite for a dog. We had Bonnibel in the house, Linda in the studio, and in their different ways they lavished their love on Bill. He returned it in a manner that delighted them.

November 3, 1947

This day I begin work with the idea that has been teasing my mind for months. I have been reading a great deal about mental illness. I've had time to think. Now that my pencils are sharpened and a pad is under my hand, I hope words will come. I have the title, Beloved Bondage. *Perhaps that's enough for one day.*

November 20, 1947

The work goes slowly these days as I feel my way, seeing the story that is in the idea. The background is all there, and the characters, but I've not been quite sure where it is going. Then suddenly, today, I saw it clearly—the three stories, John's, Althea's, Louisa's, three approaches to the same problem. I have dwelt with it so long that now it is clear in my mind. I seem to be listening and taking down what I hear. In Nearby, *I wanted to expose and then extinguish prejudice, so in this book I want to let in light that there may be more understanding of people who suffer mental illness.*

After talking with a psychiatrist, and with a nurse in a mental hospital, I begin to feel sure of my direction. I look forward to their help when the story is ready for checking. The doctor said an amazing thing, that 90 percent of the people confined to state hospitals have become the way they are because of selfishness. That bears out my feeling about Althea's condition.

December, 1947

I had two days in New York, seeing friends and publishers. Mr. Coward took me to luncheon at the Yale Club. I told him about the story, a bit fearfully and breathlessly, but his interest was keen and kindly. He felt that this book would be a real turning point for me and said that his firm intended to get back of it and do everything to establish it. He liked my three-way approach, but thought I had set myself a hard task. "But novel writing is hard," he said, and smiled as if to comfort me. He asked if I would like an advance and I said no thank you, not until I had a typescript on his desk.

"And when will that be?"

I couldn't say for sure.

December 31, 1947

My year-end task: adding up in my little ledger the moneys received. This time the total is in five figures.

1948

AMOS AND VIOLET

January 2, 1948

*Back at my desk and hoping for long uninterrupted hours.
Mr. Coward would like to have the finished work sometime in
April. Can I possibly do it? Part One, John's story, about 35,000
words, is done.*

January, 1948

The middle part was the most difficult, but in three
weeks that was done and I could swing into Althea's
story. The words came so quickly that I could hardly
bear to stop writing. It was not easy to sleep; so much
that wants to be said kept tumbling through my mind.

To understand Althea better, I took a course in rug
hooking at the Sharon Arts Center on Thursday evenings. For three hours I sat at my frame, as did six other
people at theirs, with strips of colored wool slowly
being drawn into patterns. Our instructor was wise and
gentle. She helped me keep the finished design always
in mind while I approached it slowly. A murmur of
conversation flowed around the room. How different

this creativity is from that of a writer, working alone and always in quiet. Doing this made me feel like Althea, growing strong in herself as she worked out of herself.

February 19, 1948

It is 6 P.M. and I've been at my desk all day, since Bill left for Concord after an early breakfast. He has a talk to give tonight in the north country, so he and T.K. will not be back until tomorrow. Now I can say that the last words have been written. I have been tired often during these weeks, but there is no feeling like this, for suddenly there is nothing more to say, and nothing more in me. A pile of manuscript pages, something like 90,000 words, looks up at me from my desk.

March 1, 1948

My goal is to revise twenty chapters in as many days, and somewhere in the middle of the revising, I'll start typing the first chapters.

March, 1948

The first part, John's story, was revised and typed. A copy went to the psychiatrist for her checking. These were days of unremitting work, nights of broken sleep, as it all kept going over and over in my mind. Sections came back from the doctor and they carried her "approval of your theme and its outcome." The nurse cheered me after her first reading. "It was a difficult assignment you elected for your talents, but I had no fear of the outcome. It took the Yates balance of head and heart—of sensitive discernment and sympathetic writing—to handle well such a subject."

April, 1948

On this perfect spring day when there was a sense of the newborn everywhere, *Beloved Bondage* was finished. All the typed pages went into a box, wrapped and addressed to Mr. Coward. I got it to the post office minutes before the last mail went out. Alleluia!

May, 1948

Mr. Coward phoned me. He liked it, the Althea parts especially. He suggested a few changes which I could easily make and send the new pages down to him.

Two weeks later Mr. Coward had another feeling. He thought the three approaches were not good and that the whole story should be rewritten. I gave his comment deep and earnest thought, then explained my feeling in a letter to him. To change so radically would be to write a whole new book, and this I could not do.

How easily editors use the telephone! In ten days Mr. Coward called. Astonishingly he agreed with me. The book was to go through as I wrote it, as I saw it. A contract would be in the mail within the next few days. Did I wish to have a dedication? If so, it was to be sent soon, as they were moving right ahead with production. I sent it, and it was an impersonal dedication but one deeply felt—*"To all librarians; especially to those who have helped me through the years and who, by their own love for books, have guided me into high and happy adventures."*

Dedications are such a meaningful way of repaying indebtedness. Two books were dedicated to Bill, *Patterns* to my mother, and *Mountain Born* to my father.

158

I had to accept the fact that giving talks is as much a part of a writer's life as answering letters, for requests came to me from schools and clubs and libraries, all sorts of groups. Some want to make dates as much as a year ahead. I accepted what seemed right and reasonable, and what fitted in with the life of Shieling. As with everything, I asked Bill for help. He had done much speaking during his business career, and it was part of his work as he made the N.H.A.B. known throughout the state.

He reminded me of my lessons with Edith Clements during that first year in London: to stand tall and breathe from my toes, to hum frequently and feel the resonance, to loosen my tongue with exercises like "Peter Piper picked a peck of pickled peppers" and "Sister Susie's sewing shirts for soldiers."

"Ten people, or fifty, or five hundred in your audience," he said, "it makes no difference. Find one who appeals to you, preferably in the last row, and direct your words—not your gaze—to that person. Weave your humor in with the whole. Don't tell a story just because it's funny, but because it fits."

He held up his right hand, fingers wide spread. "There are really just five things for you to remember, not like a memory exercise, but build them into you so they become part of you." As he enumerated, he took one off each finger.

"Think what the occasion demands and plan accordingly. Write your talk first, then make a brief outline on three-by-five-inch cards and have them to refer to so you won't wander. Drive into your subject at the start and find a point of contact with your audience. Enjoy the telling; if you do, they will enjoy the listening. And it's like writing, stop when you've said what you had to say."

He dropped his hand. Five fingers had done their work, but he had one more point to make, "Be yourself."

"What if my knees shake?"

"Let them shake. It's your voice that matters."

When people come up to me after a talk, just looking into their smiling faces gives me a feeling that the borders of friendship are constantly widening. Sometimes it's an autograph people want, and here I have my rule: gladly will I sign one or a dozen books, but not little slips of paper.

July, 1948

Lillian came for three days. I still marvel at the way editors came to visit, but she had reasons—to talk with Nora and Bill about *Andy,* and to bring me up to date on the books I've done for her. We did enjoy each other. She brought with her a copy of *Publishers Weekly* in which Coward-McCann had a full-page announcement of *Beloved Bondage.*

On Friday we took Lillian to the Amos Fortune Forum, a lecture series given in the old Meeting House in Jaffrey Center and named after a notable citizen of a century or more ago—a freed slave. We got there early. It was a lovely evening, and I suggested going out to the graveyard to see the stone that marks Amos Fortune's grave, but Lillian and Bill were comfortably settled and already deep in conversation. So I went alone. In the gentle evening, with the light beginning

to deepen beyond Monadnock and a late thrush singing, I read the words on the stones of Amos and his
wife, Violet, and thought what an accounting, lives so
simply lived, so complete! And yet I wanted to know
more.

How? Why? What? Pursuing me were the questions that pursue the mind of a writer and will not let
it rest until they are answered. Eight strokes sounded
from the great clock on the spire of the Meeting House
so I went back to join Lillian and Bill, but I didn't hear
a word of the lecture. My mind was full of the man for
whom the lecture series had been named.

Before Lillian left for New York, she asked me if
I had anything in mind. I said yes, but that it might deal
with the later years of an old man. Would young people
ever be interested in such a book?

She said, "Young people are interested in character
wherever, whenever, it appears. Age does not matter if
the story is a living one."

Lillian wrote in our guest book, "To come to Shieling is like coming home."

August, 1948

So. She who walks like a teacher has become a
teacher!

Asked to conduct a workshop at the University of
New Hampshire's Writers Conference, I was tempted
to say no to the director, Carroll Towle. I wondered if
I could ever fulfill such an assignment. Then I realized
that the request wouldn't have come to me if I couldn't
do it, so I accepted. After all, there was no work on my
desk calling for attention, Nora was part of Shieling
and would assume my responsibilities, Bonnibel had

no puppies on the way, and the garden at the midpoint of summer was able to take care of itself. I arrived in Durham on the first Sunday of August, ready to take up my duties, but feeling very scared and green. However, I talked with the poet Rolfe Humphries, who was also lecturing at the conference, and after that I was a different person.

"Be yourself. Give them what you are. If you find that what they have submitted to you is not of the first order, get them to talk about themselves, draw them out. There is always a potential. Look for and develop it." Then, as if he had not said quite all, he added, "It may surprise you what they reveal and you discover."

After I got to know Rolfe better, and as a colleague, I stirred up my courage to show him some of my poems. He read them slowly, then asked me what I thought of them.

"I suppose they're just jingles, really."

"Oh no, they are like you. They have delicacy and dignity. But how seriously do you take them?"

I had to say not very, that my novels were my main interest and always would be.

He didn't say anything in particular when he handed my papers back to me. If he had, it would have been words like those Mr. Coward used, "Stick to your last."

The two weeks at the conference included morning lectures, reading of manuscripts submitted, individual meetings with the students, and an evening talk. Some work turned in to me was good, some was not, but in each piece and in every person there was always something that could be seriously considered. At the end I was tired, almost beyond refreshing. But Carroll Towle renewed me. "Your sincerity and capacity to inspire have been invaluable," he said. "Will you come back next year?"

September 23, 1948

Beloved Bondage has arrived, the first copy, mine. Two colors predominate and they are my favorites—blue for the binding, brick for the jacket. Nora did the design, and the two heads, John's and Althea's, are beautiful. How the title stands out in Nora's calligraphy! The book, even on the outside, looks like a mature piece of work. It has a feeling of substance. Tonight I have the greatest of all joys: I start reading it aloud to Bill.

October, 1948

A telegram came saying that the People's Book Club had taken Beloved Bondage. *Mr. Coward said he couldn't be more pleased. Nor could I.*

The reviews were good, strong and reassuring. *The New York Times* had said of *Nearby* that I wrote "shining prose warmed by strong conviction and gentle faith." Then the *Boston Herald* was saying of *Beloved Bondage* that it "has a transcendent quality of spiritual values which gives it a deeper meaning and validity." There were some reviews that were acidulous, but I thought they were from people who did not understand it. More important than the reviews were the letters that came, especially those that said, as one did, "This has helped me to live my life."

The family urged me to come to Buffalo, and I did, for two days. The life at Hillhurst was filled with the old joys, and there was, as well, an autographing party at a bookstore, some picture-taking, and a radio interview. Yet so much was the same. On the train back I made this notation in my Think Book: "Remember the wisdom of not going public where family can congregate. They will never see you as the world does, and nothing is gained by taxing their credulity. Meet them on your own ground at Shieling as much as possible; elsewhere only if the need is imperative."

November 6, 1948

A day to remember, and the twelve red roses were more meaningful than ever. Bill said, "Do you realize that you have that many books now bearing your name?"

1949

IMPRINT OF A MAN

Winter, 1949

The idea that took hold of me last summer as I stood by the two headstones in the little graveyard in Jaffrey Center would not let me go. There was a story if I could find my way into it. I did the reading available, two chapters in the *Town History*, but there was so much more I wanted to know, needed to know. What had Amos Fortune's life been before he purchased his freedom and came to Jaffrey to establish himself as a tanner? Tanning was a subject about which I knew little, and there would be much reading ahead of me if I were to establish some kind of background.

First, I wanted to make sure that I would not be trespassing on another writer; so I queried many people —citizens of the town, ministers, retired professors living in the area—and always I was given the same answer: "But there's nothing known about him, only those last twenty years of his life that are in the *Town History*."

I had a persistent feeling that though nothing was known, much could be found out about this man who

165

was "born free in Africa a slave in America . . . purchased liberty professed Christianity lived reputably and died hopefully." He was no ordinary man. His memory had left an imprint, but he himself had left a sum of money "for the school." The modest amount has increased with the years, but the Amos Fortune Fund is still carried in the town books and used in some way from time to time, in Amos Fortune's words, "as the town sees fit to educate its sons and daughters."

The road was mine to follow, and no bird dog on a scent was more determined than was I.

From the public library in Jaffrey and from the State Library in Concord, I gathered books for a winter of reading: *The Negro in Colonial America; Rum, Romance and Rebellion; Social History of New England; From Slavery to Freedom; Negro Musicians and Their Music.* I found a book about early methods of tanning. Old newspapers gave me nothing about the man, but a great deal about the times in which he lived. I knew that his will was on file in the Cheshire County Courthouse in Keene. I knew that the house he built on the bank of Tyler Brook was still lived in.

I commenced a search back to the towns in which he had lived before he had come to Jaffrey. Town clerks were helpful and interested, opening to me the vital statistics of years long past. When I came upon his name, it was like a handclasp across the years. With his will in my hands, I could see what possessions he had and how he disposed of them, and I could run the tip of my finger over his own signature. Among those who helped me was Evelyn Ruffle, the librarian in Jaffrey. She finally discovered the whereabouts of his papers that had been "lost" for half a century: his freedom paper that was his passport to life as his own man; the bills of sale for Lydia and Violet; the indenture paper for his Negro apprentice, Simon Peter; and one for the white boy, Charles Toothaker; the neat receipts he gave to people and requested of them. All these were found and, even more, they could be handled and studied.

I often went by the small house he had built for himself and Violet, but I never asked to go in, for at that time it did not seem quite right. I knew where the pool was in the brook, where he had soaked hides before tanning them. The Meeting House where he had worshiped, though no longer a place of worship, was familiar to me. And, to keep contact, I would go to the graveyard to stand by the stones, classic in their simplicity, equal in height, slim slate stones that had taken the weather since 1801, as he had taken the weather of his ninety-one years and Violet, her seventy-three.

Sometimes a friend would ask me what I was doing with myself, and my reply was the brief one, "Reading." Yes, it was a winter of reading, note taking, thinking.

Bill knew of my search and comforted me, so did Nora, and Lillian was always the prod. When I told her in desperation at the beginning that there was so little to go on, she insisted there was plenty. "What you don't have at hand you can find out."

I was doing exactly that, and the fragments were beginning to fit together like the pieces of a puzzle.

Reading books about the slave trade harrowed my heart, and there were many times when I wondered if I could possibly go on.

"Watch out," Lillian said in her commanding way, "or you'll be writing a tract about man's inhumanity, and where will that get you? You have a story to tell, tell it."

She was right and all my instincts said to me that the story was the account of a man living his life against great odds and triumphing over them. I climbed Monadnock and measured myself against the mountain, as he must have done while living in its shadow: great mass of rock shaped by aeons of time, great man shaped by the events of his life, both looking skyward. And as the weeks went on, I felt that I knew this man.

There was much I could put together from what I read and from the countryside, which is mine as it was his, and from the clues I followed that took me to the wharf at Boston where he was sold as a slave and given his name; but I had to imagine the life in Africa. My first chapter would be built from what I read about the tribal customs, the conditions, the raiders, the journey across the Atlantic. A high pile of books stood on one side of my desk, a small pile of notes on the other. When would I know I had enough background? When would I begin to write?

May, 1949

Spring came slowly, with much cold and grayness, but with a beauty of bud and blossom and birdsong that seemed unlike anything before. The crabapple tree was a fountain of bloom. The swallows filled the air with their exultation, then dove into the barn on family business. And suddenly I was ready to write! The reference books went back to the libraries that secured them for me. I had all I needed in my notes, and perhaps more than I needed in my heart. This had happened to me before. I should trust and know that it will always happen. When a story is ready to be written, the words will be there.

Lillian asked Nora to do the illustrations, and, though Nora was involved in other work, she began some preliminary sketches—the house in Jaffrey, the church, the stones, tanning tools. She climbed Monadnock for views she would need. She could do a great deal even before she had a draft from me to work with.

So I started to write and it all came together. When summer intervened, I would put it away for a while. The time between would give me a perspective.

Summer, 1949

The days are long and light. Bill is home more and we have time to talk. When we first met we so often talked about God—the Being that transcends and enfolds all religions, the Being beyond all churches and creeds. I keep wondering what I believe. Bill makes it all so simple.

"There's only one relationship—ours to God. There's only one Way—living love."

I talk about creeds and their formalities, inwardly resisting them.

"Why do you feel so driven?"

"Because I must be honest with myself." As soon as I say that, I realize that one can impale the spirit on such determination.

"The manner by which the Way is found," Bill reminds me gently, "is not so important as living the Way."

"Creeds help, don't they—shaping, guiding, preparing us?"

"Yes, of course, but they can confine, too, putting limits on that in man which should always keep expanding and growing."

I didn't say anything.

"You'll work things out for yourself, you always do, and then you'll put what you've found into your next book."

How well he knows me!

And so we go on, never wanting to arrive at any conclusion, for that might terminate the search, the reaching. Bill has gone

*much further along the Way than I have—the tenor of his life
shows that. I seem to have to keep finding things out for myself,
holding to what is right for me just as I hold to what is right for
my books.*

*The past months I have been so filled with Amos and his
search for freedom, the way he was compelled to give it to others after
he had secured it for himself. What gave him such persistence?
Could it not have been part of his search for the reality of God?*

July, 1949

Bill had a project which he hoped to work on
sometime. It was a book, of course. He and Nora spent
hours talking about it and planning the illustrations. It
grew from a hump in the lawn between the house and
the barn, the hump is Old Joe. In the days when our
Shieling was a working farm, Joe was one of the horses.
Every day he delivered milk in the village, becoming so
accustomed to the route that, even without words from
the man who walked beside him or held the reins, he
would stop and go forward again from one house to the
next. No doubt he had many rewards: pats, a carrot, a
lump of sugar, and the kind of words an animal thrives
on.

Joe was only five or six at the time of the Civil
War, when the need for horses was great. He was mus-
tered into service, wounded, hospitalized, returned to
service. After Appomattox he was honorably dis-
charged, was returned to Peterborough, and resumed
his milk route as if he had never been away. He lived
to a good age and, always having been a part of the
family, was buried between house and barn.

Something about Old Joe appealed to Bill, and

Nora, too, and they were confiden† about getting him into a book. Old Joe became a part ⌐ ¬ur family philosophy of always having somethin †head to look forward to.

August, 1949

After my first week at the University of New Hampshire I could say that the Conference was more exciting than the year before and I felt much more competent. There were many new students, but those from last year had tales of work sold and were eager to show work in progress. The hours were long, the reading voluminous, but I would not have had it otherwise. I recalled something James M. Barrie once said: "Work is never hard unless you'd rather be doing something else." Next to writing myself, there is nothing I would rather do than help people with their writing. It's a challenge to me as much as to them to direct them to the stories that need to be told, the stories that they can tell.

October, 1949

After three months away from my desk, I came back to Amos. There was much to be done, but the work was all there, and it read better than I thought. The time away mellowed it, but it also showed me places where I could tighten, and other places where a thought could be further developed. A small, but to me important, bit of new material came to light about Amos' wife, Violet. It gave more meaning to the words about her on the slate headstone: "By marriage his wife by her fidelity his friend and solace." Nothing could hinder me now until I came to the end, the closing period of his life, and the title was there, the title that says it all, *Amos Fortune, Free Man*.

December 15, 1949

The finished pages went to Lillian today. It has been tremendous to do. I have felt so close to a man whose humility and love for others shone like beacons.

December 20, 1949

Editors have a curious way of showing approval. Lillian telephoned to say that my typescript had already gone into production and that the title was right for the story. Would I be able to read the galleys soon and when would Nora send her finished work?

December, 1949

I told Bill of a dream I had, one of those dreams that are so filled with color and so uncluttered that they do not disperse on waking, but stay with all their clarity into the morning and so into forever. I was an archer with bow in hand and a quiver full of arrows over my shoulder. There was a target—gold, red, blue circles, and, in the center, the bull's-eye was black. I fitted an arrow into my bow, drew the cord, let the arrow fly, and it went to the bull's-eye, to the very center.

"Some dreams are hard to interpret," Bill said, "this one is easy."

"What do you mean?"

"You'll see."

Year's End, 1949

Hungry for a holiday, we went to Williamsburg for Christmas—the Yule log, the wassail bowl, the fragrance of many candles, the warmth of great fires, the sight of cardinals on a lawn dusted with snow, and Nora describing it all to Bill as only an artist can. The week crowned the year for each one of us.

1950–1951
A NEW VOICE

January, 1950

On the grayest of gray days with a cold rain falling I began to write the *Olive*. It had been in the back of my mind ever since I discovered Roxbury Center, a wooded hilltop where all that remains of a once-thriving community are cellar holes. There is a small white church, where dried and faded ropes of ground pine spoke of Christmas services, and there is a well-kept graveyard. On the slate stones the name Freelove appears often. It was clearly a feminine family name, and I speculated on the tenderness of its early meaning. Once I had my setting, and that unusual name, the characters began to form in my mind, gathering their own identities.

I called it *Thou, Being a Wild Olive* from that allusive verse in Romans (ch. 11:24): "For if thou wert cut out of the olive tree which is wild by nature, and wert graffed contrary to nature into a good olive tree; how much more shall these, which be the natural branches, be graffed into their own olive tree?" I had a feeling that Mr. Coward would want a title better suited to a novel, and if he didn't, the trade department would. And that would be all right. After all, I had only to write the book, they would have to sell it, and a title goes a long way in that direction. This was a story that would embrace some of the conflicts and struggles that I'd recently been through within myself, struggles to know what I really believed. But it was also about country things and a deep, pure love.

February, 1950

Back to the *Olive,* but I did have to take some time off to read the galleys on *Amos.* It's exciting when a story is ready to be written, what happens—often unexpectedly. It was becoming Benedict's story—the influence of his life, the riches of its lovingness on one particular person. I'm not always sure, at this point, where I'm going, but I trust the idea to develop itself.

April 3, 1950

Nearing the end. Chapter twenty-five, and now I ask myself is it all just words—400 pages, 80,000 words—or have I really said something?

April 5, 1950

On this raw and misty day I write the last lines, now for the hard part—the revision: the part I like best of all.

April, 1950

Lillian telephoned to say that *Amos Fortune* had won the *Herald Tribune* Spring Festival Award as the best book for older children. The presentation would be in New York on May 5, and this time I must come down to receive it and the check myself. When Bill got home from Concord and I told him he said, "Remember your dream?"

May, 1950

Home again after such a satisfying two days—one given over to Lillian and the *Herald Tribune,* the other to Mr. Coward. When I met Mrs. Van Doren and accepted from her the check, we both recalled the day in 1929 when she had given me some books to review. "I can see you've been broadening your field," she said. I agreed, "But you helped me get started." I felt as grateful for that good memory as I was for the check that I held in my hand.

The next day was with Mr. Coward. I had two chapters of the *Olive* typed and an outline for the rest. He liked it, all but the title, and planned to make it their fall fiction if I could have it all to him by the end of May. The calendar told me I would have twenty-six working days, it almost seemed impossible: but, given a challenge, anything is possible. We discussed titles. The one I used was the scaffolding and its only purpose was to support the story.

"How about *City on a Hill*? Or *A Lantern Only*?"

Suddenly *Guardian Heart* came out of the blue nothing, as titles often do. It says what the book is, and we both liked it. He insisted on giving me an advance, and the check is in four figures.

"But it isn't all typed," I remonstrated.

He smiled. "It will be."

June, 1950

At 1:35 A.M. June 3, I finished the typing and got my box of many pages in the mail when the post office opened. I missed the date agreed on by a few days but had been assured that it would not matter.

October 1, 1950

Guardian Heart was published on the twenty-ninth of September, and today there is a full-page ad and a super review in the Herald Tribune. *Mr. Coward telephones to say that the* Christian Herald *Family Bookshelf has taken the book for their January selection. My cup runneth over.*

October 15, 1950

How is it that I feel at such a low ebb—wondering if I've ever written anything worth reading, wondering if I'll ever write anything again? Everything gets harder to do. Nothing is easy.

"Why, Bill, must this be so?"

"Because your standard keeps going up. You'll never be entirely satisfied. You wouldn't want to be."

We're cutting a new trail in the woods. When I can't get anywhere with words, I put my pencil down, pick up my brush cutter and hatchet and head for the woods. Working hard and being able to see accomplishment helps me get level with myself again.

Perhaps I am in a fallow time. If that is good for the land, it must be good for the mind.

November 6, 1950

Red roses, yes, but a necklace of golden links, too; more than a manifest of twenty-one years, they are a symbol of forever.

A Christmas letter from Martha came to fill in the time we've been out of touch with, but never unaware of, each other. "You know of my marriage in Buffalo in 1928 to the handsome Dutchman, Franciscus Visser 't Hooft, a graduate of Delft University with doctor's degrees in Science and Engineering. Presently he is president of a chemical company here in Buffalo. For some years I was a veritable Mother Hen with two daughters and a son, so my descent into the New York Art World was delayed. I now have a big studio outside the house which enables me to spend hours alone and undisturbed to paint, and the family are encouraging and supportive. I've been exhibiting all along, winning numerous awards and feel that I am well on my way as you are. I'm sending you an invitation to my second solo exhibition at Contemporary Arts Gallery, Inc., New York. Being with this gallery has opened the opportunity of being selected for many national exhibitions as well as future ones at the Whitney and other museums, with a possible purchase by the Whitney. Little did we dream, during those early days in New York, where our paths would lead us, but both of us followed a vision: hard work and self-discipline, obtaining some of our goals. You have been painting pictures with words, I with my brush, and we'll continue to tap our creative energies with excitement. And so, back to my easel!"

It was one of the days when Bill worked at home and I was glad, for how could I have stood it if he had not been here? I was in the kitchen making a birthday cake for a young friend of ours who was having her party at Shieling that afternoon, February 16. When the mail came, Bill went out for it. He came into the kitchen with it in his hands.

"Something important for you, I had to sign for it."

It was a letter with the gold of a Special Delivery stamp on it, from an address in Portland, Oregon, and the name of someone in the Children's Library Association. I opened it, wondering why anyone so far away should be in such a hurry. I couldn't believe what I was seeing until I read it aloud to Bill.

"*Amos Fortune* has been given the Newbery Medal as 'the most distinguished contribution to American literature for children.' "

Oh!

We called to Nora, we put the kettle on, and the dogs danced around us in excitement. We moved into the sunny living room, read and reread the letter, poured cup after cup of tea, and rejoiced. The medal belonged to us all: to Bill, whom I had thanked in the acknowledgments "for the confidence he gives me when I assign to myself what seems to be an almost impossible task." To Nora, to whom the book is dedicated, "dear partner in many books and good friend through the years." Her sensitive, careful illustrations

179

brought Amos and his time alive and made the countryside real.

Then the telephone rang. It was Lillian, telling me that, though the news was not to be made public until May 5, and the medal not to be presented until July 10, I must start now writing my acceptance speech. *The Horn Book* would need to have it by April to be printed in the July issue.

"How can I ever do anything so far ahead?"

Her reply was crisp, "You can."

"What do I say?"

"The road you have come by, the way you went about doing *Amos.*"

The cake did get finished, the little girl had her party, and when she blew out the candles, no one wished harder than I in my joy that her wish would come true. When I went to bed that night, still almost unbelieving, words of my old friend, George MacDonald, kept coming to me, "It's just so good it must be true."

March, 1951

To New York for the gathering in Mr. Melcher's office with just the few concerned there and several librarians. Katherine Milhous who was to receive the Caldecott Medal for her book *The Egg Tree* was there with her editor; Lillian and I for the Newbery. There were congratulations all around and many kind words were said, pictures were taken, and reporters asked questions that the editors were better able to answer than the medalists.

When Lillian saw me off on the night train for

Boston, she said, in that no-nonsense way of hers, "Now, write your speech."

I felt as though the latent fires in me had been kindled, for ideas that had been in the back of my mind were all coming forward, and I wanted to write them. Bill was as firm as Lillian. "Do what you must do first and get that speech done. What you want to do can come later." So I worked on the speech, going way back into my childhood with its desire to write and coming up through the years. I described the search for Amos' story, and inevitably my own philosophy crept in. There was only one possible title: Climbing Some Mountain in the Mind.

Bill, too, had an assignment from *The Horn Book*, and he spent hours on it. T.K. typed it and Bill didn't show it to me until it was all finished.

"Oh, Bill, you've remembered so much about me, about our life."

"Just some important things. I couldn't cover all our years."

"It doesn't have a title."

"Title enough," he said.

So our work was done and the two papers went to *The Horn Book* in good time.

The news was getting around, for letters were crowding the mailbox, and I must take time to answer them. They were from all kinds of readers—young people, of course, but teachers, and ministers, some of my students from the University of New Hampshire, and many friends. One from a twelve-year-old boy in the Midwest gave me utter joy. "Amos Fortune must have been a great guy. Did you know him?"

Did I!

April 1, 1951

Lillian tells me there are three thousand copies of Amos Fortune, Free Man *at the Colonial Press in Stow, Massachusetts, waiting to be autographed. They have been ordered by libraries all over the country. I am to do them as soon as possible. Writing my name 3,000 times? Why, I could write a whole story with that number of words. It is less than an hour's drive to Stow and through pleasant country. The Press has set up a table for me in a corner where I can work. It is stacked with books; as they are done more books are brought on large dollies.*

April, 1951

It took me three days. Stopping for an hour at noon to eat my sandwich and limber my fingers, I could not do more than a thousand a day. It was an experience. As I wrote my name, I tried to think how special each book would be to a particular library, to the children who would read it, but by the end of the third day I had to hold on to myself to keep from writing it wrong —Amos Yates did not look right, nor did Elizabeth Fortune.

"You've earned a treat," Bill said, so we combined a day in Boston, when he had an appointment with Dr. Barton, with a swan boat ride and luncheon at the Ritz.

After Bill's time, Dr. Barton asked to see me alone. I thought he wanted to give me some special word about Bill, but it was me. He didn't like the swelling on my throat and said I was to come down to the Hahnemann Hospital in Boston as soon as he could make the arrangements.

"But I can't. I have an important speech to give in Chicago in July."

He was firm. "I will explain to Bill." He did when we went out to the waiting room.

Bill was wonderful. He seemed to understand much more clearly than I what Dr. Barton was saying, what it might mean or not mean, and when we left the office I felt his courage becoming mine.

May, 1951

I was in the hospital four days and when I got back to Shieling it was with a bandaged neck and a voice like a whisper. Dr. Barton had told Bill and assured me that the tissue was benign and there was nothing to be concerned about. "Let your strength be your guide," he said to me.

So there I was, feeling like royalty as I sat in the garden and was waited on. The weakness I knew at first was beginning to go and every day strength came back to me like an incoming tide. But energy, where was it? I couldn't have written a page if I tried, but I could rest in the realization that the acceptance speech was written a month ago.

The garden never seemed more lovely, the birds more songful; perhaps because I was sitting in it, not working in it. The dogs cozied up to me. Nora brought cups of tea. Bill read aloud from his braille books. When I was by myself I had on my lap those typed pages, and I familiarized myself with them so that when the time came to give the speech it would roll from me as easily as talking.

June, 1951

Nora and I went to Boston and Dr. Barton checked the healing of the scar. He said there was no need to wear even a small bandage now. He was proud of his work. I know how he felt. I am proud of mine when I send a good-looking typescript off to an editor. Then Nora and I went shopping for the dress I would wear at the banquet on July 10. We found it—long, pale green, with the simplicity that is elegance. The neck is just slightly open, giving room for the gold-link necklace Bill gave me on our anniversary and which covers what is left of the scar.

July, 1951

There is always a train letter or a boat letter or a flight letter for the one leaving Shieling from those staying home. So when I tucked myself into my little roomette, with the wheels of the train purring through the darkness, I had two letters to read. Nora's was filled with joyous love and assurances that all would be well at home while I was away. She ended with those remindful words of Benjamin Whichcote's, "It is the chiefest of all Good Things for a Man to be Himself."

Bill's letter was quite long, written in soft pencil on his raised-line pad. It was not always easy to read, but I did not miss a word and I hugged his thoughts to my heart.

"... You are on your way to the ALA and the Newbery Award. To many, this important event whereby you receive this high recognition will seem as

184

if a new and shining light in the literary heavens had come into focal view. To those who really know you and who have seen you climbing, climbing up the steep trail, it seems more as if you had come to an altitude where the morning sun had found you and revealed you to the many who had not discerned you before. And what do they see? A young woman, youthful but mature, radiating health, strength, poise, modesty, joy, and a deep-lying inner oneness with her world and her Creator. They will not see the years of eager striving, listening, mastering of self and craft. They will see and feel the results . . . people may say you are going to Chicago to receive something. Actually you are going to give, to give more of yourself to more people than ever before. It is a part of your steady climb on the upward trail."

The two days before the program were filled with parties and people and bookstores and all sorts of lovely attentions, but Bill had made me promise to have some "do-nothing time" every day for myself, and I did. He also told me that on the afternoon of the banquet to go to the ballroom where it would be held, ask to see the microphone, and test it to be sure I would feel easy with it. I did. When I went up to my room to change, I thought of all that Miss Clements had told me about deep breathing to get richness into my voice, and those little exercises to limber lips and tongue. When it came time to meet Lillian and move into the evening, I felt ready and calm inside, and exactly right in my new dress.

It was a huge room, that ballroom of the Palmer House. There were twelve hundred people, librarians mostly, editors, publishers, and many who had to do with books in some way. It was all very festive, and people looked their best and happiest. The dinner was delicious, and it was pleasant to have conversation with the guests on either side of me at the head table.

The presentation of the medals and the speeches came after the dinner, and Katherine was first. Her words and her person brought ringing applause. Then Mr. Melcher spoke my name, and I took the few steps that brought me close to him and to the microphone. He said some very nice words when he put the medal in my hands. What could I say but "Thank you." There was applause, then silence, and that silence was my cue.

Standing before the microphone, I felt perfectly comfortable with it as it was in the same position that I had practiced with earlier in the day. I had my pages in a red leather folder, which I placed on the stand before me, but, except for an occasional dropping of my eyes to them, I looked out into all those friendly faces and spoke to them. The words were there, just as when I write on paper the words are there, and my voice seemed strong to me, and sure. Sometimes there was laughter and that gave me a chance to swallow and take a deep breath, and when I spoke of Amos, especially toward the end, there was something very deep. I could feel it coming back to me from that room filled with people.

Later, someone asked, "What do you do with a medal?"

There is no answer, for it is what a medal does to you. I see it as a trust, a symbol, of better work to be. I end these notes as I ended my speech, "And so I go on climbing."

BIOGRAPHICAL NOTE
BY WILLIAM McGREAL

It must have been in the fifth Newbery Year that I met Elizabeth Yates. It was at a party in New York. Behind her slightly shy brown eyes there was a seriousness not wholly concealed by a frequent twinkle. "Small talk" was not her forte. When she spoke, it was of things she felt. She was forthright. I liked her. We made a date.

The following Saturday found us atop Timp, one of the so-called peaks in the Hudson Highlands. Our campfire had died down to embers. Elizabeth closed the little worn volume she had brought in her knapsack and leaned back against the ledge. After a moment she said, "That's good writing. Someday I, too, shall write something good." I felt no need to respond. We sat for a long time looking across the foothills.

And now we are in the thirtieth year of the Newbery Award. The recipient is Elizabeth Yates. She is my wife. That "someday" for her has come.

In her books there are many evidences of the good writer, and I frequently have the joy of seeing them before they reveal themselves on the printed page. As my thought turns back over the years to recall the path along which she has climbed, I find myself thinking not so much of writing landmarks as of inner qualities and outward signs.

It was no doubt during that happy day on Timp that I first saw many qualities of the real person—a love of mankind and nature; a zest for the outdoors and high places; a courage and stamina; a striving and searching. Then followed the intervening years of work and accomplishment, of travel, adventure, and growth; and now we find ourselves happily content with the deepening roots of our life in the hills of southern New Hampshire. Here at Shieling, "our shield, and

Condensed from *The Horn Book Magazine*, July 1951. © The Horn Book, Inc.

shelter," Elizabeth the countrywoman is truly at home. Here she finds elements that speak to her in her own language—the brown earth, the tumbling brook, the woodland trails, the rising hills, the grazing sheep, the open fire, the stimulating friends. And for all these she gives a full return to her home, her community, and, through her books, to an ever-widening circle.

Elizabeth is tall and slender. She has a stout heart and a strong body. Her hair is as brown as her eyes. She likes tweeds, salads, mountain climbing, reading aloud, spaghetti, lively discussion, walks in the rain, children, animals, house guests. She dislikes frills, waste, taking taxis, gossip. She has no feeling for arithmetic and her interest in domestic mechanics is nil. She has plenty of courage, a strong faith and a native expectancy of good. Living with her is a high adventure.

When confronted by a challenge or faced by a danger she is at her best. Her resourcefulness and courage filled a need more than once when we were climbing in Switzerland or on a pack trip in Iceland. About eight years ago, this steadiness of spirit had to meet a different kind of crisis when I lost my sight. Not once did Elizabeth falter. There was no tragedy, no defeat. Though the adjustment seemed so very slow at first, I gained hope and confidence as I felt her closer companionship, her strong hand in mine and her unconquerable spirit. Quietly and swiftly she took over tasks I had formerly done around the place; brought in the firewood, mowed the lawn, even swung the scythe. It became her pleasure to do all of the evening's reading aloud. It was her fortitude and philosophy that carried us through the deepest waters and that continue to strengthen and sustain. Now that the inner vision is clearer and I am again enjoying a sense of usefulness and activity, I can cherish even more the stout heart, the hand that became my hand, and the sight that became my sight.

And yet, during these years, she has managed somehow

to nurture and respond to her own creative spirit.

Elizabeth has reliable intuitions and successfully bases her action on them even when logic disapproves. She prefers to make quick decisions and get things done. She has learned to make minutes count. In running what I call a three-ring circus—our home, the garden, and her writing—she has had to be efficient.

All household tasks are not necessarily pleasurable, but long ago Elizabeth developed the practice of finding some satisfaction in each job no matter how monotonous. Often when I hear her singing herself through a task I suspect that she is thus making a tough undertaking pay dividends. On the shelves in our cellar there is a rainbow of her handiwork. From our garden she captures for our winter pleasure beans and corn, beets and tomatoes, relishes and preserves; from the nearby mountain slopes come blueberries and blackberries in abundance. A cool corner holds onions, marrow and her favorite, winter squash.

Though our farmhouse is small it is adequate for our needs, and as Elizabeth abhors clutter she does not readily acquire new things unless they are to fill a definite purpose. This simplified living of hers springs from a simplified philosophy. She is an unusual combination of the ideal and the practical.

Elizabeth has learned through experience that only she can determine just what she wants to say; so she has learned also to seek her own counsel and stand fast by her own decisions. She feels that she knows her own limitations and capacities, and is constantly striving to lessen the former and enlarge the latter. It has been a joy to me to observe the steady unfolding and deepening of her experience and wisdom.

Her heart is with the basic qualities of human life, and because there once lived in a nearby village a man who cherished and practised these qualities, Elizabeth wrote the story of his life. That it is well written we know, for in this year of 1951 the Newbery Medal has been awarded to *Amos Fortune, Free Man.*

AUTHOR'S NOTE

The Lighted Heart (Dutton, 1960; Bauhan, 1974) overlaps this story in that it spans the years from approximately 1935 to 1960 without identifying them on the calendar or by locale. It has an ample cast, but only the main characters—Bill, his wife, Elizabeth, and the dogs—have their actual names. The reason is that this is the story of Bill McGreal, his loss of sight and gradual adjustment to a new way of life and usefulness in work for the blind, and of his wife, who understood and helped. It is a book of country joys and sorrows, of friends and adventures. It could happen anywhere to any two people.

The "Mary" in the book is the friend, Nora Unwin, who became part of the life at Shieling; to have identified her would have meant describing her as the artist she became and would have involved events in the world at the time. "Dan" is a composite of three neighbors, all farmers, who brought practical knowledge, and much more, to the story. Other characters, though real, are not given their actual names for the same reason that Mary is fictional.

The concern of *The Lighted Heart* is not happenings in the world, as in this book, but domestic events, and the purpose is to show how two people met a challenge, at a midpoint in their lives, and came through it with deeper understanding and faith. It is all true, but done with broad sweeps and reliance on a writer's "license" to make changes when needed. When a draft was read to Bill, he was highly amused. "Did I really say that?" I would remind him of the occasion, and then he would often enlarge on it.

ONE WRITER'S WAY is as close to true events in the world as notes, letters, research, and memory can make it, showing the growth of my writing life.

BOOKS BY ELIZABETH YATES

1938 *High Holiday*. London: Adam & Charles Black. Repr. 1945.

1938 *Gathered Grace*. Cambridge: W. Heffer & Sons.

1938 *Hans and Frieda in the Swiss Mountains*. London: Thomas Nelson & Sons, Ltd.

1939 *Climbing Higher*. London: Adam & Charles Black. Published 1940 under the title *Quest in the Northland*, by Alfred A. Knopf.

1941 *Haven for the Brave*. Alfred A. Knopf.

1942 *Under the Little Fir*. Coward-McCann.

1942 *Around the Year in Iceland*. D. C. Heath & Co.

1943 *Patterns on the Wall*. Alfred A. Knopf.

1943 *Mountain Born*. Coward-McCann.

1945 *Wind of Spring*. Coward-McCann.

1947 *Nearby*. Coward-McCann.

1947 *Once in the Year*. Coward-McCann.

1948 *Beloved Bondage*. Coward-McCann.

1948 *The Young Traveller in the U.S.A.* Letchworth: Phoenix House. Repr. 1955.

1950 *Guardian Heart*. Coward-McCann.

1950 *Amos Fortune, Free Man*. Aladdin Books. Repr. 1967 E. P. Dutton & Co.

1950 *Children of the Bible*. Aladdin Books.

1952 *Brave Interval*. Coward-McCann.

1952 *A Place for Peter*. Coward-McCann.

1953 *Hue and Cry*. Coward-McCann.

1954 *Rainbow Round the World*. Bobbs-Merrill Co.

1955 *Prudence Crandall, Woman of Courage*. Aladdin Books. E. P. Dutton & Co., 1955.

1956 *The Carey Girl*. Coward-McCann.

1958 *Pebble in a Pool: The Widening Circles of Dorothy Canfield Fisher's Life*. E. P. Dutton & Co. Published 1971 under the title *Lady from Vermont*, by Stephen Greene Press.

1960 *The Lighted Heart*. E. P. Dutton & Co. Repr. 1974 by William L. Bauhan.

1962 *The Next Fine Day*. John Day Co.

1962 *Someday You'll Write.* E. P. Dutton & Co.

1964 *Sam's Secret Journal.* Friendship Press.

1964 *Carolina's Courage.* E. P. Dutton & Co.

1964 *Howard Thurman, Portrait of a Practical Dreamer.* John Day Co.

1966 *Up the Golden Stair.* E. P. Dutton & Co.

1966 *Is There a Doctor in the Barn?* E. P. Dutton & Co. Repr. 1977 by William L. Bauhan.

1967 *An Easter Story.* E. P. Dutton & Co.

1968 *With Pipe, Paddle and Song.* E. P. Dutton & Co.

1969 *New Hampshire.* Coward-McCann.

1969 *On That Night.* E. P. Dutton & Co.

1971 *Sarah Whitcher's Story.* E. P. Dutton & Co. 2d ed. 1979 by Regional Center for Educational Training.

1973 *Skeezer, Dog with a Mission.* Harvey House.

1973 *The Road Through Sandwich Notch.* Stephen Greene Press.

1974 *We, the People.* Countryman Press. Repr. 1976 Regional Center for Educational Training.

1976 *A Book of Hours.* Vineyard Books. Repr. 1983 by Seabury Press.

1977 *Call It Zest.* Stephen Greene Press.

1978 *The Seventh One.* Walker & Co.

1981 *Silver Lining.* Phoenix Publishing.

1981 *My Diary, My World.* Westminster Press.

1983 *My Widening World.* Westminster Press.

1984 *One Writer's Way.* Westminster Press.

Books Edited by Elizabeth Yates

1940 *Piskey Folk: A Book of Cornish Legends.* John Day Co.

1942 *The Doll Who Came Alive.* John Day Co. Repr. 1972.

1947 *Joseph.* Alfred A. Knopf.

1949 *The Christmas Story.* Aladdin Books.

1949 *The White Ring.* Harcourt, Brace and Co.

1953 *Your Prayers and Mine.* Houghton Mifflin Co. Repr. 1982 by Friends United Press.

1963 *Sir Gibbie.* E. P. Dutton & Co. Repr. 1979 by Schocken Books.

OXFORD MONOGRAPHS ON SOCIAL ANTHROPOLOGY

General Editors

MAURICE FREEDMAN B. E. B. FAGG

A. C. MAYER E. ARDENER